Friendship or Enmity?

Friendship or Enmity?

The Christian and the World in the Letter of James

by VINCENT HIRSCHI

RESOURCE *Publications* • Eugene, Oregon

FRIENDSHIP OR ENMITY?
The Christian and the World in the Letter of James

Copyright © 2019 Vincent Hirschi. All rights reserved. Except for brief quotations in critical publications or reviews, no part of this book may be reproduced in any manner without prior written permission from the publisher. Write: Permissions, Wipf and Stock Publishers, 199 W. 8th Ave., Suite 3, Eugene, OR 97401.

Resource Publications
An Imprint of Wipf and Stock Publishers
199 W. 8th Ave., Suite 3
Eugene, OR 97401

www.wipfandstock.com

PAPERBACK ISBN: 978-1-5326-9398-4
HARDCOVER ISBN: 978-1-5326-9399-1
EBOOK ISBN: 978-1-5326-9400-4

Manufactured in the U.S.A. OCTOBER 30, 2019

Ἐδίδαξας δέ σου τὸν λαὸν . . . ὅτι δεῖ τὸν δίκαιον εἶναι φιλάνθρωπον
—Wis 12:19

Dieu seul est juste et humain (. . .)
Et nous, pourquoi avons-nous séparé le juste et l'humain,
la pureté et la tendresse?
—Eloi Leclerc

Contents

Acknowledgements | ix
List of Abbreviations | xi

1 Introduction | 1
2 Κόσμος in the Epistle of James | 10
3 Friendship with God and Friendship with the Κόσμος in James | 42
4 The Role of the Church in the Letter of James | 68
5 Conclusion and Implications | 99

Appendix | 105
Bibliography | 113
Scripture Index | 123

Acknowledgements

THIS BOOK IS THE fruit of the work done for my ThM thesis. The initial aim was to compare James 4:4 and 1 John 2:15-17, two passages that have much in common and are often cited as parallel in commentaries. I wanted to understand better the similarities and differences in their attitude towards the world. Yet, as my research progressed, I found myself more and more drawn to the letter of James for its own sake. Soon enough, what had started as a comparison became a study on James's epistle.

I hope that, despite the academic format, my excitement for the subject can surface in these pages, and that the reader will be as interested as I was to discover some of the riches hidden in this short epistle.

I am especially thankful to Mariam Kovalishyn for her support and for sharing with me her passion for the letter of James. I am grateful for her readiness to direct this project even though it ended up encroaching on a sabbatical and a maternity leave! She has been supporting this thesis from its inception to its conclusion. I deeply appreciated the help she provided in helping me organize my thoughts in writing, spending significant time to offer detailed comments on the drafts of these chapters. Finally, I am also indebted to her openness, honesty, and humour when speaking about the joys and challenges of the bookish life of a scholar. I am also indebted to George Guthrie for being the second reader of this thesis, and for providing so many helpful comments and wise advise. I learned a great deal from him, both as a scholar and as a person. My thanks also go to Rikk Watts, who influenced me more than anyone else at Regent College. Although he had no direct influence on this thesis, his approach to Scripture influenced every paragraph of my exegesis. I am especially beholden to him for his invitation to marvel in the depth of the relationship between the Old Testament and the New. May his example of holding together intellectual honesty and spiritual passion have a lasting impact on my studies. I want to thank Sven Soderlund for his repeated encouragement: I rarely met someone in whom grace and truth are so wonderfully weaved together. Lastly, my deepest gratitude goes to David Clemens who instilled in me the appreciation for Greek. It was an honor to study and then assist him. The depth of analysis I found in his classes have taught me more about exegesis than I could tell.

On a more intimate level, I am thankful for my wife Carine and the support she provided at so many different levels. I thank her for her patience with me and with my work, for the discussions and suggestions, for her corrections and her support. To my children Matthieu, Benjamin, and Yohan: you made sure my life was rooted in reality. Thank you.

Most of all, I thank the one who gave me breath and Spirit. May my work be for your glory and my life for your joy. May your two hands, your Word and your Spirit, shape me in such a way that I may share your life, and share it with those you place around me.

List of Abbreviations

AB	Anchor Bible
ANF	The Ante-Nicene Fathers
AOTC	Abingdon Old Testament Commentaries
BDAG	Walter Bauer, Frederick W. Danker, W. F. Arndt, and F. W. Gingrich. *Greek-English Lexicon of the New Testament and Other Early Christian Literature*. 3rd ed. Chicago: University of Chicago Press, 2000.
BECNT	Baker Exegetical Commentary on the New Testament
BHGNT	Baylor Handbook on the Greek New Testament
BSac	*Bibliotheca Sacra*
BST	The Bible Speaks Today
BT	*The Bible Translator*
BTB	*Biblical Theology Bulletin*
BZAW	Beihefte zur Zeitschrift für die alttestamentliche Wissenschaft
BZNW	Beihefte zur Zeitschrift für die neutestamentliche Wissenschaft und die Kunde der älteren Kirche
CBQ	*Catholic Biblical Quarterly*
CRINT	Compendia rerum Iudaicarum ad Novum Testamentum
ETR	*Études théologiques et religieuses*
EvQ	*Evangelical Quarterly*
ExpT	*Expository Times*

LIST OF ABBREVIATIONS

FC	Fathers of the Church
HNTC	Harper's New Testament Commentaries
HTR	*Harvard Theological Review*
HvTSt	*Hervormde Teologiese Studies*
IVPNTC	The IVP New Testament Commentary Series
JBL	*Journal of Biblical Literature*
JECS	*Journal of Early Christian Studies*
JPS	Jewish Publication Society
JSJSup	Supplements to the Journal for the Study of Judaism
JSNT	*Journal for the Study of the New Testament*
JSNTSup	Journal for the Study of the New Testament: Supplement Series
JSP	*Journal for the Study of the Pseudepigrapha*
JTSA	*Journal of Theology for Southern Africa*
LBS	Library of Biblical studies
LCL	Loeb Classical Library
LNTS	Library of New Testament Studies
LSJ	Henry George Liddell, Robert Scott, and Henry Stuart Jones. *A Greek-English Lexicon*. 9th ed. Oxford: Clarendon, 1996.
NCBC	New Cambridge Bible Commentary
NIBC	New International Biblical Commentary
NIDNTTE	*New International Dictionary of New Testament Theology and Exegesis*
NIGTC	The New International Greek Testament Commentary
NovT	*Novum Testamentum*
NovTSup	Supplements to Novum Testamentum
NTR	New Testament Readings
NTT	New Testament Theology
NTS	*New Testament Studies*
RevExp	*Review and Expositor*

RHPR	*Revue d'histoire et de philosophie religieuses*
RB	*Revue biblique*
SBLRBS	Society of Biblical Literature Resources for Biblical Study
SBLSP	Society of Biblical Literature Seminar Papers
SNTSMS	Society for New Testament Studies Monograph Series
SP	Sacra Pagina
SUNT	Studien zur Umwelt des Neuen Testaments
TDNT	*Theological Dictionary of the New Testament*. 10 vols. Edited by Gerhard Kittel and Gerhard Friedrich. Translated by Geoffrey W. Bromiley. Grand Rapids: Eerdmans, 1964–76.
TNTC	Tyndale New Testament Commentaries
TOTC	Tyndale Old Testament Commentaries
TynBul	*Tyndale Bulletin*
WBC	Word Biblical Commentary
WUNT	Wissenschaftliche Untersuchungen zum Neuen Testament
ZECNT	Zondervan Exegetical Commentary on the New Testament
ZKG	*Zeitschrift für Kirchengeschichte*
ZNW	*Zeitschrift für die neutestamentliche Wissenschaft und die Kunde der älteren Kirche*

1

Introduction

READERS OF JAMES'S EPISTLE are faced with an intriguing puzzle. On the one hand, James displays great awareness of the social implications of the gospel. He insists that Christian faith is active, and especially that those who profess faith must demonstrate it with love for the vulnerable. The importance of caring for the poor is emphasized in James more strongly than in any other book of the New Testament. On the other hand, James impels his readers to reject "the world." James's readers discover that "the world" possesses a defiling influence and that friendship with it must be shunned. The question then must be asked: how is it possible for James to hold these two positions at the same time? This book attempts to answer this question. In other words, we propose to study James's understanding of the role of the Christian in relation to the world.

There are at least three reasons to undertake such a study. First, care for the poor and rejection of "the world" are two central ideas of James's epistle. Consequently, no satisfying grasp of James's theology is possible unless one gives a coherent account of the way these ideas relate and influence each other.

Second, there is a surprising dearth of studies devoted to the relationship between church and culture that anchor their argument in Scripture. Several important monographs approaching the problem from the point of view of systematic theology have been published in the last fifty years, but none approaching the topic from Scripture itself.[1] Even though different biblical authors take different views on that issue, it would be helpful to have studies analyzing those views as a first step toward providing a comprehensive biblical theology of church and culture. This book proposes such an analysis of the letter of James.

Third, this topic is one of the most important issues for the church today. In my estimation (resting only on my personal experience, but informed by twenty years of lay involvement in six different churches in four countries and three continents), churches usually stress one side of the tension at the expense of the other. Some emphasize rejection of the world without seeing the importance of being a blessing for society; others become so involved in society that speaking about any kind of differentiation from—let alone condemnation of—"the world" is either uncomfortable or impossible. Of course, these are caricatures, extreme attitudes rarely met in real life. Nevertheless, the actual practice of many churches is sadly all too close to one of these caricatured stances. When the latter view is embraced, the church risks losing the uniqueness of her contribution by subverting the message she is called to proclaim. When the former view is adopted, the church is in danger of withdrawing into an ivory tower. This usually happens in one of the following ways. A church can protect itself so well from external influences that it turns a deaf ear to the divine commission sending it into the world. Such a church has been blinded to the need of those who do not belong to it. Another common attitude is to limit the church's role to the "spiritual needs" of people. In that case, the church will care for the spiritual needs of its members and attempt to convince outsiders that they, too, have deep spiritual longings, even though they may not be aware of it. Unfortunately, these churches most often respond to questions and issues that are not those of their neighbors.

Neither of these positions do justice to the biblical text. The church needs a theology that affirms both sides of this tension *at the same time*. The fact that care for the poor and rejection of "the world" are both stressed in James's epistle suggests that James does *not* call his readers to strike the right

---

1. Oliver O'Donovan grounds his argument in the development of the biblical story and thus represents a partial exception. See O'Donovan, *Desire*. New Testament scholars have devoted significant effort in recent years to examining the ways Jesus's lordship challenged Roman political ideology. However, these studies usually focus on the political challenge of the gospel. The differences between politics in the first century and the modern state make it difficult to move from the conclusions of these works to a theology able to inform the church today.

balance between keeping their distance from society and being sufficiently involved with it. Rather, he urges Christians to develop, fully and uncompromisingly, two apparently opposed attitudes: repudiation of what he calls "the world," and active compassion for the poor.[2] According to James, fully embracing these two poles is necessary to participate in God's redemption of the creation. If James is right, the church will be able to play its role only insofar as it understands what it is called to reject and to embrace.

STRUCTURE

The exposition of this thesis is divided in two parts. The first two chapters define what "friendship with the world" means in James's letter, and the third develops the positive role of the church towards society and creation. A conclusion exposes the implications of this study for a biblical theology of the church and the world.

The second chapter proposes a detailed exegesis of all the passages in which the noun κόσμος appears. Each verse will be analyzed in its literary unit, with a view to understanding how κόσμος is employed throughout the epistle. James uses the word in a very consistent manner to depict a value-system grounded on prestige and wealth. "The world" always stands for a system of value that does not take God into account, rejects his commands, and does not trust in his promises. In particular, it is a value-system that negates the centrality of the command to love one's neighbor. The rejection of "the world," therefore, is not a denial of earthly life, of the created order, nor of human society. Rather, to reject "the world" means to free oneself from a corrupt worldview and value system that poisons human relationships, thereby making it possible to build a community that reflects God's character and functions as a foretaste of his kingdom.

Chapter 3 discusses φιλία as it was understood in the first century. Since the concept of φιλία was common and well developed in the first century, we will explore its meaning in pagan and religious literature of the time. Even though modern and ancient friendship overlap, the classical commitment to friendship was stronger, more specific, more codified, and more tied to ideas of honor and identity than friendship in its present

---

2. Some may argue that these two things are not opposed to each other: that is, that the church must separate itself from society and then care for the material needs of those who belong to the church. If James indeed advocates a sectarian position, there is no tension at all between care for the poor and condemnation of "the world." As we will see, however, this position does not do justice to the text.

form. A solid grasp of this concept is, therefore, essential to understanding the force of James's argument. I will show that friendship included the notion of deep commitment and sharing of the same mindset. It follows that "friendship with the world" stands for agreement with the views held by the κόσμος and a readiness to organize one's life according to these principles. Given the nature of "the world," rejecting friendship with it is James's way of referring to the hatred of evil. As for "friendship with God," it is the ideal James invites his readers to pursue.

In Chapter 4, we will analyze the role of the church throughout James's epistle. I will propose that James expects the church to play three different roles. First, she is called to be a foretaste of God's kingdom. As such, she must be a community where relationships are organized around the values of Torah and in which the plight of the poor is relieved. Second, the church has a prophetic role to play in the culture, in that its presence is a warning sign to everyone that God will soon come in judgment. Third, James believes that the health of the church is, in some ways, related to the restoration of creation. This is one of the main reason James insists so strongly on the theme of wholeness and purity within the church.

The concluding chapter will summarize the development of the thesis and provide a synthesis of the different elements discovered in the process. These final thoughts will offer five implications for our understanding of the relationship between the church and the world.

PREVIOUS SCHOLARSHIP

To my knowledge, nobody has studied in-depth the relationship between James's social imperatives and the command to reject friendship with "the world." Several monographs on different aspects of the letter inform the argument, however. Studies on the meaning of κόσμος in James have been completed by Luke Timothy Johnson and Darian Lockett.[3] Chapter 2 will draw from them both, but the major part of the research comes from various commentaries. The influence of the *topos* of friendship in James has been the subject of a recent study by Alicia Batten.[4] Chapter 3 will draw heavily on her study, but take it in another direction. Batten contends that the language of friendship functions as an invitation to the congregation

---

3. Johnson, "Friendship," 202–20; Lockett, *Purity and Worldview*, 107–45.

4. Batten, *Friendship*. Batten's article on friendship and patronage is also important, albeit to a lesser extent. See Batten, "Patron or Benefactor?," 257–72.

to stop relying on patronage and rely exclusively on God. In my view, this proposal does not sufficiently take into account the way "friendship with God" is pictured in other Jewish works, the fact that Abraham is depicted as a friend of God, nor the importance of the link between friendship with God and mature faith. For these reasons, I propose that James employs the language of friendship in another way. Concerning the topic of Chapter 4, William Baker and Richard Bauckham have studied James's understanding of the church's role in society.[5] Baker's study focuses on the specific shape and organization of the community but does not provide much material for James's theology. Bauckham's chapter provides a richer analysis, and the research proposed here is in line with his own conclusions. In some areas, however, this thesis either completes Bauckham's picture of the church or finds additional elements that strengthen the ideas he laid out.

LIMITATIONS

The research presented below is primarily based on scholarship written in English. A few commentaries published in German and in French have been consulted when possible, but only to a limited extent. Research written in other languages has not been taken into account.

This study focuses exclusively on the letter of James and will not attempt to move beyond a coherent account of the relationship between church and culture in that letter. It would be fascinating to bring the conclusion of this study into dialog with similar projects on other biblical books, but that is for another time.

WORKING ASSUMPTIONS AND METHOD
Authorship and Date

Since nothing in this thesis depends on one's view of authorship or date of writing, these matters do not require a detailed discussion. Scholars agree that the appellation "James" refers to James the Just, the brother (or half-brother) of Jesus; nobody else was famous enough to be unambiguously identified by this name alone. The question, then, is whether the letter is authentic or pseudonymous.[6] For reasons well summarized by other schol-

---

5. Bauckham, "James, 1 Peter," 153–66; Baker, "Community," 208–25.

6. For summaries of the usual arguments in favor of pseudonymity, see Allison, *James*, 3–6; Dibelius, *James*, 18–19; Reicke, *Epistles*, 4; Laws, *James*, 38–42; Edgar, *Social Setting*, 223.

ars, the present author considers the former option more likely.[7] Therefore, I will simply refer to the author of the epistle as "James" throughout this thesis. Since James the Just was put to death in Jerusalem around 62 CE, an early date for the epistle follows.

Genre and Audience

It is widely accepted that James's epistle belongs together with wisdom literature.[8] Consequently, I agree with those who argue that the topics addressed in the letter do not respond to specific situations but instead represent general teaching. For this reason, the use of diatribe in the letter is taken to be "pedagogical and hortatory rather than polemical."[9]

Moreover, the address to "the twelve tribes in the diaspora" (1:1) is best understood as bearing primarily a geographical sense rather than metaphorical one. James likely wrote to churches composed of Jewish Christians or a mix of Jews and Christians living outside of Palestine, either in a specific region or in a larger area. In either case, the letter would address a group of churches rather than a single community.[10] Given the likelihood that James did not write his letter with a unique community in view, and given the complete lack of concrete evidence outside the text of the letter, it is doubtful that an attempt to reconstruct a precise historical setting would illuminate the text. Accordingly, no such attempt will be offered.

---

7. Luke Timothy Johnson provides a good summary of the arguments in favor of traditional authorship: "All the usual criteria for positing a late dating for New Testament writings are absent: there is no institutional development, no sense of tradition as a deposit, no polemic against false teachers, no highly developed Christology, no delay of the parousia. On the face of it, everything in the letter suggests an early dating rather than a late one." Johnson, "Social World," 110. For scholars who hold this position, see Davids, *Epistle of James*, 22; Bauckham, *James*, 22; McKnight, *James*, 38; Blomberg and Kamell, *James*, 35; Adamson, *The Man*, 24; Brosend, *James and Jude*, 30; Moo, *James*, 31; Cheung, *Genre*, 52.

8. Cheung (*Genre*, 5–52) provides the best discussion on the topic.

9. Cheung, *Genre*, 51.

10. This has been argued by Tsuji, *Glaube*; Bauckham, *James*, 11–28; Verseput, "Genre and Story," 96–110; Keith, "Les destinataires," 19–27. Other scholars see "diaspora" as simply referring to a group of churches outside of Palestine, but not as a sign that James's epistle was meant to be a circular letter. See Davids, *Epistle of James*, 64; Blomberg and Kamell, *James*, 35; Moo, *James*, 33; Stulac, *James*, 15. Finally, others argue for a pseudepigraphic writing in the genre of a diaspora letter. See Allison, "Fiction," 529–70; Kloppenborg, "Diaspora Discourse," 242–70.

Given that the letter's opening identifies its readers with the people of Israel, James's letter is best read with a Jewish background in mind. Methodologically, this implies that Jewish history and traditions will be more important than insights from Greco-Roman cultural background. In this, we agree with Hartin, who stresses "how vital an understanding of the world of Judaism is for understanding the letter."[11] Studies focusing on Graeco-Roman culture and rhetoric are certainly useful as well, but our first reflex should be to inquire about the ways in which Jewish tradition and beliefs shape the text.

Structure and Exegetical Methodology

The structure of James's letter has been debated at length, but no consensus has emerged so far. For this reason, the argument of this thesis will not be rooted in any specific outline of the structure of the epistle. This is not to say, however, that the organization of James's material is irrelevant.

In his influential commentary, Dibelius famously wrote that "eclecticism is an inherent aspect of paraenesis," so that it would be fruitless to look for an overarching logic organizing the book.[12] However, despite a lack of consensus on the overarching structure of the book, it is widely accepted today that the epistle comprehends several coherent and carefully built self-contained units.[13] In these sections, the argument is well-organized and intelligible, the fabric of the text is tightly-knit, and the connections between the different parts are strong. Arguments have even been advanced to show that James was well versed in rhetoric and that some of these sections were organized according to fixed patterns of argumentation.[14] Sections that do not follow a typical rhetorical pattern also possess inner logic.[15] Despite the lack of a clear overall structure, the letter is marked by a strong coherence of thought.[16]

---

11. Hartin, *James*, 74.

12. Dibelius, *James*, 8.

13. For a survey on the major proposals for the structure of the epistle, see Taylor, *Text-Linguistic Investigation*, 8–34.

14. Advocates of this position have pointed to Jas 2:1–13; 2:14–26; 3:1–12. See Watson, "James 2," 94–121; Aletti, "James 2,14–26," 88–101; Watson, "Rhetoric of James 3:1–12," 48–64.

15. See, for instance, the argument in Johnson, "James 3:13–4:10," 327–47.

16. See the argument in Bauckham, *James*, 61–69.

Two practical consequences for the way the exegesis is performed follow from these observations. First, a proper exegesis must take into account the whole unit in which a verse is set. In other words, understanding the argument of the whole pericope is essential to grasping the meaning of one verse. Hence, the verses about the world that we examine will be discussed in the context of their literary units. Second, since these units are set together in a coherent composition, it is also assumed in what follows that each section affects the other parts of the letter. In short, the whole epistle will be considered to be a well-thought-out literary artifact, and it will be assumed that repetitions of words or thoughts from one section to another imply (or at least possibly imply) that the two passages should inform one another.

Intertextuality

James manifests an obvious interest in grounding his argument in the Jewish Scriptures. But this interest is not always made completely clear. Besides a few quotations (Lev 19:18 in 2:8; Gen 15:6 in 2:23; Prov 3:34 in 4:6) and the explicit references to four exemplars of faith (Abraham and Rahab), patience (Job), and prayer (Elijah), the letter is steeped with allusions to the biblical text. These range from clear echoes to more faint ones.[17] Since James appeals to Scripture in an oblique way at times, often invoking a biblical passage or concept without clear lexical parallels, we need to pay careful attention to possible allusions.[18]

Taking seriously the genre of James's letter (wisdom literature) implies that James hoped that his readers would not only read his letter but meditate on it, maybe even memorize it. Indeed, this is a general feature of wisdom texts.[19] Furthermore, James himself stresses the importance of listening, remembering, and practicing. James 1:22–25 speaks first and foremost about hearing and applying Torah itself, but it no doubt also illuminates the way James expects his readers to hear his own message. James certainly expects his readers to ponder the text carefully and to tune their

---

17. Some of the clearest allusions are to Jer 9:23–24 in Jas 1:9; Isa 40:6–7 in Jas 1:10–11; Deut 5:17–18 in Jas 2:11; Isa 5:9 in Jas 5:4; Jer 12:3 in Jas 5:5. A host of other potential but more debatable allusions can be found.

18. For an example of allusions with little textual parallel, see Johnson, "Leviticus 19," 391–401.

19. Cf. typically Ps 1:2; Prov 2:1–5.

ears so as to discern the ways in which James rephrases the message of those who spoke the same wisdom before him.

This thesis will therefore consider quotations and allusions to the OT as hints pointing toward other possible implications of the text. The term "quotation" refers to places where James cites Scripture in an unmistakable way; the terms "allusion" or "echo" will be used where he alludes to a biblical text in an oblique way. No formal distinctions will be drawn between "allusions" and "echoes." Although there is something to be said for distinguishing between these two words (allusions are usually defined as being clearer than echoes and present in the mind of the author), there are two reasons to avoid differentiating between them here. First, this thesis aims to gain a better understanding of the *message* of James, not of the way James produced his letter. Recognizing where James grounds his argument in the Jewish Scriptures is fundamental to proper exegesis, and it is sometimes interesting to establish the degree of influence a given source had on an author,[20] but neither of these things is the goal of the present thesis. Second, the distinction between "allusions" and "echoes" is subjective and can easily become arbitrary. A continuum clearly exists between obvious allusions and more ambiguous ones, but it is precisely that: a continuum. In what follows, I will use "echo" and "allusion" as synonyms. When an allusion serves as illustration or support, little more than a mention of it will be offered. When, however, important elements are derived from a possible OT allusion, I will provide an argument defending the reasons for granting that allusion a larger part in the interpretation.

---

20. Patrick J. Hartin, for example, does this with the saying of Jesus in James's epistle. Hartin, *James and the Q Sayings*.

2

Κόσμος in the Epistle of James

INTRODUCTION

IF OUR AIM IS to understand what "friendship with the world" means for James, we have to begin by ascertaining the meaning of "friendship" and "the world" within the context of James's epistle. This chapter will analyze the way James speaks of "the world," and the next will develop the concept of friendship.

The term κόσμος can mean many things. In classical Greek, its primary meaning is that of order. The other connotations of the word derive from this one.[1] Κόσμος also signifies adornment (since the beautiful is defined as what is well ordered) and the material universe (given its perfect ordering). Although the LXX maintains these various meanings, the sense of adornment almost disappears in the NT.[2] At the same time, the word gained new meaning. In the NT, κόσμος usually stands for one of three things: a physical place, either the whole universe or, more narrowly, the inhabited earth; humanity in general; or the system on which human existence is built.[3] This last sense is almost always negative, describing humanity's existence in a state of rebellion against God.

---

1. See LSJ, s.v. κόσμος; Sasse, "Κοσμέω κτλ.," 3:867–98.
2. This sense appears only once in the NT (1 Pet 3:3).
3. For more information on the way the word is used in the NT, see Bratcher, "Meaning of Kosmos," 430–34; Sasse, "Κοσμέω κτλ.," 3:867–98.

The polysemy of the word κόσμος makes it necessary to consider in detail James's uses of the word. If James uses it to refer to a physical place or to humanity, one would have good reason to suspect a sectarian stance in James. Some commentators take exactly that approach, viewing the opposition to "the world" as a sign that James has no interest in seeing the community involved in society.[4] I propose that this view arises from a misreading of James.

James employs the word κόσμος in a consistent way, and since it appears only five times, it is possible to analyze every verse in which it occurs.[5] The aim of this chapter is to discuss each occurrence in detail and then briefly analyze Jas 3:15. Even though that last verse does not contain the word κόσμος, the clear dichotomy between earthly and divine wisdom adds important elements to the present discussion. Our goal is to understand not so much a word, but a worldview. For James, "the world" describes a whole set of values and a way of being that takes root in them. It is that set of values that we seek to understand and describe.

ΚΌΣΜΟΣ IN JAMES 1:26–27

The word κόσμος appears for the first time in Jas 1:27, the closing section of chapter 1. It is widely accepted that Jas 1 functions as an extended introduction to the letter and that Jas 1:26–27 serves as a hinge. These two verses are also often seen as "a way of conceptualizing the entire letter's ethical position."[6] For this reason, and because of their aphoristic nature, these verses need to be read with the rest of the letter in mind, allowing the context of James to unpack in greater detail what he here compressed in a few words.

In this passage, James does two things: he contrasts two ways of serving God, and gives a definition of pure worship.[7] Both elements are central

---

4. The question of James and sectarianism will be discussed below in the section on James's view of the church. On James lacking all sense of Christian responsibility towards society, see Keith, "Les destinataires," 24. On James as taking a sectarian position, see Perdue, "Paraenesis," 241–56; Perdue, "Social Character," 26; Wall, *Community*, 98–101; Elliott, "Holiness-Wholeness," 71–81.

5. The word κόσμος appears five times in four verses: 1:27; 2:5; 3:6; 4:4 (x2).

6. McKnight, *James*, 162.

7. The contrast between "vain worship" and "pure worship" is emphasized by bringing the two phrases side by side. The first appears at the end of 1:26 and the other appears at the beginning of 1:27.

to James's thought. The whole letter aims to help people move from vain to pure worship and to exhort those who are already engaging in pure worship to perseverance. James 1:26–27 thus possesses a central place in James's theology.

The structure of the pericope is that of two self-standing aphorisms, but the unity of theme invites the reader to read each verse in light of the other. "The aphoristic form of each [verse] invites the reader to ponder each for its own sake, while the text's placing of the two beside each other invites further reflection on their relation to each other."[8] Hence, although the word κόσμος only appears in 1:27, verses 26 and 27 will both be discussed below. Since the section summarizes chapter 1, I will also assume that the preceding verses help us to understand Jas 1:26–27 properly.

> Εἴ τις δοκεῖ θρησκὸς εἶναι
> μὴ χαλιναγωγῶν γλῶσσαν αὐτοῦ ἀλλ' ἀπατῶν καρδίαν αὐτοῦ,
> τούτου μάταιος ἡ θρησκεία.
> θρησκεία καθαρὰ καὶ ἀμίαντος παρὰ τῷ θεῷ καὶ πατρὶ αὕτη ἐστίν,
> ἐπισκέπτεσθαι ὀρφανοὺς καὶ χήρας ἐν τῇ θλίψει αὐτῶν,
> ἄσπιλον ἑαυτὸν τηρεῖν ἀπὸ τοῦ κόσμου.

> If anyone supposes to be religious
> while not bridling his tongue but deceiving his heart
> this person's religion is vain.
> Pure and undefiled religion in the sight of God and Father is this:
> to look after orphans and widows in their affliction,
> to keep oneself unstained from the world.[9]

---

8. Bauckham, *James*, 70–71.

9. All translations from a Greek text are mine unless otherwise specified. Five variant readings appear in each verse, but only one of these ten variants impacts the interpretation of the verse. 𝔓⁷⁴ reads "to protect them from the world" (ὑπεράσπιζειν αὐτοὺς ἀπὸ τοῦ κόσμου) instead of "to keep oneself from the world." Some scholars, including David J. Roberts III, P. Trudinger, and Elsa Tamez believe this version to be original. Matthew Black, on the other hand, sees that variant as a later modification, but "a particularly happy one." All these authors dislike the NA28 reading because they understand the idea of "keeping oneself from the world" as a call to physical separation from society. This, however, is a mere assumption. Nothing in the epistle of James itself encourages this reading. The variant is only attested in one manuscript (𝔓⁷⁴), and there is no good argument for considering it superior to the other reading. The arguments for taking 𝔓⁷⁴ as the original reading have been analyzed and answered by Bruce C. Johanson, and will not be discussed further here. See Roberts, "Definition," 215–16; Trudinger, "Down-to-Earth," 61–63; Tamez, *Scandalous Message*, 16; Black, "Critical and Exegetical

Vain Worship, Loose Tongue, and Deceived Heart

James 1:26 presents speech as the litmus test of pure religion. The message of Jas 1:26 is clear enough: in God's eyes, controlling the tongue is a non-negotiable part of pure religion. Although the verse itself does not explain the importance of holding one's tongue—no doubt because of the pithiness that gives the verse its rhetorical power—the rest of the letter enables us to get a good sense of James's rationale behind this statement. Holding one's tongue is central for two reasons: speech reveals the hidden state of the heart, and pure speech is essential to maintaining peaceful relationships in the community.

Transformation and Deception

In Jas 3:2, James claims that the person who controls the tongue is able to control (lit: "to bridle," χαλιναγωγέω from χαλινός, a bit or bridle) the whole body.[10] As Adamson puts it, "if a person can control the most recalcitrant of his members, he can also control his other members."[11] Hence, by speaking of bridling the tongue in 1:26, James singles out the most difficult element in the practice of faith. But James goes even further than that: controlling the tongue is not the most difficult thing to do—it is impossible.

Indeed, Jas 3:8 claims that the tongue cannot be tamed or subdued (δαμάζω) by human beings. This leads us to the paradox that the religious person *has to* accomplish the impossible task of controlling the tongue. The only way out of this dilemma is to recognize that "on the human level it is impossible to control the tongue, but with the help of the wisdom from above (3:17) it is possible."[12] It follows that James sees pure religion as enabling the faithful to live in such a way that the evil tendencies of human nature are overcome. For James, faith in God is either transformative or dead.[13]

Here we should carefully consider the import of the theme of deception, picked up in 1:26, especially since it has already appeared twice in the

---

Notes," 39–45; Johanson, "Definition," 118–19.

10. The same verb is used in Jas 1:26 and appears nowhere else in the NT.

11. Adamson, *The Man*, 370.

12. Hartin, *James*, 205.

13. James stresses this idea repeatedly, describing religion unaccompanied by a transformed lifestyle as vain (1:26), unable to save (2:14), dead (νεκρός, 2:17, 26), and useless (ἀργός, 2:20).

preceding verses.[14] Those who practice vain religion think of themselves as religious and agree with James that offering proper worship is an essential human duty. They would most likely protest James's assertion that their worship is stained and, therefore, unacceptable to God. James does not challenge their religious practices as such; instead, he critiques other habits. For him, their lack of self-restraint in their speech shows that their worship—no matter how earnest they think it is—is useless (μάταιος, 1:26). The uselessness of such religion is demonstrated precisely in that it fails to produce its intended goal: transformation of life towards righteousness (1:21). Although these people believe they are honoring God and obeying his commands, they have in reality stopped welcoming the "implanted word" (1:21), or at least refuse to act upon it (1:22). They have subverted the essential meaning of devotion to God. For James, their lives are shaped by "the world" rather than by God's word, and "the world" functions as a deceiving power blinding them to the commands of God that matter most.

Bridling of the Tongue and Covenant

To bridle one's tongue is not only a way to test whether or not one's worship is pure, but also an essential part of a healthy community life. The metaphor of bridling the tongue is primarily an image of restraint and control. Speaking of pure speech clearly recalls the ban on anger found in 1:19 ("slow to speak, slow to anger").[15] As we already noted with the language of deception, this implies that the failure to control one's tongue leads to the failure to produce the righteousness God wants (1:20). More importantly, the person who does not master his or her tongue lets it be controlled by impulses or personal desires, which James explicitly forbids. These things are, for James, at the root of divisions and fights in the community (in 4:1–2, also implicitly in 3:13–17). Indeed, most of the sins of the tongue mentioned in the letter can be summed up under the rubric of destroying the peace in the community (1:19; 3:15–16; 4:1–2, 11–12). Not controlling one's speech means allowing one's words to destroy others. Life inside the community depends on the willingness of each member to shun destructive patterns

---

14. Πλανάω in 1:16, παραλογίζομαι in 1:22. Guthrie and Taylor take "the perils of self-deception" as the main theme of Jas 1:13–27. Guthrie and Taylor, "The Structure of James," 703.

15. On the decision to read this section in relation to the preceding verses, see Amphoux, "Une relecture," 554–61; McKnight, *James*, 162–64.

of speech. Failing to do so reflects self-centered concerns and self-assertive behaviors that hinder the peace within the community.

Though the negative aspect of controlling the tongue receives more emphasis in the epistle, the positive side also plays an important role. The image of the bridle brings to mind a rider *guiding* a horse, not merely restraining it. James makes this plain in 3:1–12, where he develops the metaphor and speaks explicitly of guiding (μετάγω) the horse (3:3), and then moves to an image of a rudder guiding a ship wherever the pilot wants (3:4). It follows that bridling the tongue includes both avoiding destructive speech and using words positively to bless others.[16] Such concerns surface especially in the last chapter of the letter (addressing oaths in 5:12, prayer and song in 5:13, healing prayer in 5:14, confessing sin to one another in 5:16, and calling a brother or sister back from their wandering ways in 5:20).[17] These positive commands demonstrate the important role played by the wise use of the tongue for sustaining a healthy community. True religion leads those who practice it to care for others so that their words may build the community rather than destroy it.

Johnson shows that James's view of speech—both his negative and positive instructions—has to be understood as part of a covenantal relationship between God and the members of the community. He observes that human and divine activity are deeply intertwined in 1:19–20. Moreover, these verses are framed by two verses (1:18, 21) describing the saving power of God's word.[18] In other words, "the word of truth" (λόγος ἀλήθεια) which gave birth to the community (1:18)—and which the community continuously receives (1:21) and needs to practice (1:22)—is also that which provides the template for human speech. The word that brought every member of the community into special relationship to God defines the way community members should relate to one another. Proper speech is important because of the covenant relationship existing between God and the community.[19] James wants his community to build relationships that reflect God's character, in which every member is empowered to grow in maturity towards righteousness (1:20). In 1:26, James states that the person

---

16. *Pace* Bertram, "Ὁρμή κτλ.," 5:471.
17. Johnson, "Taciturnity," 339.
18. Johnson, "Taciturnity," 338.
19. This idea is also developed by Hartin: "James roots the whole evaluation of the need to control speech in the covenantal relationship between God and God's people." Hartin, *James*, 205.

who demonstrates a lack of care for the community by refusing to control his or her tongue moves away from a genuine covenantal relationship and embraces instead an empty, self-deceiving, religion.

Care for the Poor and Purity

James 1:27 can be read either as containing two separate ideas—taking care of the orphan and widows, and keeping oneself unstained from "the world"—or as stressing two distinct but interrelated behaviors that are unified in pure religion. It is too early in this study to answer this question in any satisfactory way, but we can nonetheless observe that since the next pericope (2:1–13) opposes κόσμος with faith and speaks of caring for the poor as the concrete expression of a heart attuned with God's, the latter option *a priori* seems better.

The first thing James asks from the faithful in 1:27 is to look after "orphans and widows," an expression that stands for the poor and helpless in society. Just as with 1:26, the aphoristic nature of 1:27 makes it difficult to specify in detail and with certainty what James means. Nevertheless, it is quite probable that, beyond his concern for relieving the plight of the poor, James also wants the community to be a place in which the quality of relationship anticipates God's kingdom. As we will see, the words used in the sentence hint at this direction, and the rest of the letter further supports this interpretation.

Calling God "Father" has become such a basic assumption of the Christian faith that modern readers risk forgetting that it was not always a common way to refer to God. For first-century Jews, speaking of "God and Father" (θεός καί πατήρ) would almost certainly evoke the idea that God is the defender of the oppressed.[20] Moreover, the connection with orphans and widows would strengthen this connection, even bringing to mind passages like Deut 10:18; Pss 68:5; 146:9. In this sense, the community is asked to defend the helpless precisely because God does so.[21] James, in other words, invites the community to imitate God's actions, and so to create a

---

20. This is the most common of the three connotations of the epithet "father" when it refers to God in early Jewish literature. See D'Angelo, "Abba," 617–21. This argument is weaker if an early date for the epistle is not accepted, since the calling God "Father" became widespread among Christians rapidly.

21. The idea that this verse implies an *imitatio Dei* goes back at least to Chrysostom. For the reference and a list of modern scholars who hold this position, see Allison, *James*, 362.

community shaped around the values that permeate God's kingdom. The verb used here to speak of caring for widows and orphans (ἐπισκέπτομαι) also supports this idea. In the LXX, it is often used for God's special care for his people or for faithful individuals.[22]

If we had no further evidence, the case would not be entirely convincing. However, the context of the verse also supports this interpretation, and even provides some detail as to how one should read that verse. In 1:9–11, James also speaks about the poor and emphasizes the theme of eschatological reversal. He contrasts the rich person who "fades away in his journeys" (1:11) and the "humble brother" (ὁ ἀδελφὸς ὁ ταπεινὸς) who receives a high position (ὕψος, 1:9). James further defines such elevation as receiving "a crown of life" (1:12). If one takes 1:26–27 as the conclusion to the double introduction of the letter, it makes sense to read 1:27 in light of 1:9–12.[23] James 1:27 functions as a summary statement that recapitulates the themes developed in 1:12 and 1:25, two passages that are textually connected.[24] Hence, by caring for the poor, the community anticipates this eschatological reversal. That this reversal is in view in 1:27 may be further indicated by the word translated as "affliction" (θλῖψις). In Scripture, θλῖψις is often used to speak of the suffering of God's people before the final deliverance.[25] Similar ideas also appear in 2:5, and they constitute an important point of James's theology.[26] In short, by caring for the helpless, James's community becomes "a counter-cultural community already living the values of God's kingdom."[27]

The other element of pure religion is to "remain unstained by the world." James employs language of purity twice in 1:27—adequate religion is qualified as being "pure," and "the world" is marked off because of its polluting influence. Purity was a central concept in first-century Judaism. First of all, being in a state of purity was necessary in order to enter the temple, which implies that no impure person could offer his or her worship

---

22. See Silva, "Ἐπίσκοπος κτλ.," 2:248–53. Hartin (*James*, 102) also believes that James uses the verb in this way.

23. Davids (*Epistle of James*, 27) proposes a similar structure. See also Francis, "Form and Function," 110–26.

24. James 1:12 and 25 each contain a blessing formula (1:12: Μακάριος ἀνὴρ; 1:25: οὗτος μακάριος—these are the only two macarisms of the letter), and the endings of 1:11 (ἐν ταῖς πορείαις αὐτοῦ) and 1:25 (ἐν τῇ ποιήσει αὐτοῦ) respond to each other.

25. See Laws, *James*, 89–90; Martin, *James*, 53.

26. See, for instance, Chester and Martin, *Theology*, 33–34.

27. Bauckham, *James*, 195.

to God.²⁸ Similarly, the parallelism between verses 26 and 27 suggests that being influenced by "the world" renders pure worship impossible.

But purity implied more than this: the consequences of one's view of purity were not restricted to the religious level. Purity "'was both a hermeneutics and social system: it formed the lens through which they saw sacred tradition and provided a map for ordering their world.' A different concept or emphasis on purity would bring about different social relationships and an entirely different way of life."²⁹ According to Darian Lockett, "purity language articulates and constructs the reality of the audience with reference to how they should relate internally and to their surrounding culture."³⁰ Consequently, an inadequate definition of purity impacts the whole of one's life, which suggests that the κόσμος describes a way of life opposed to pure worship. Since pure religion includes caring for the poor and controlling one's tongue, we can also conclude that the lifestyle promoted by the κόσμος undermines these values.

Summary

When one compares the definition of pure religion given in James 1:27 with the vain religion of 1:26, a coherent picture begins to emerge. The κόσμος is defined as a value system or worldview from which the community has to shield itself. Those who adopt this worldview will face a double consequence in doing so: "the world" will corrupt their worship, and they will be deceived in their evaluation of what matters in God's eyes. As a result, their worship will become unacceptable to God, but they will be blind to that reality. Instead of being transformed in order to grow in maturity and develop God's righteousness, these people grow more and more doubleminded, not realizing the difference between what they profess and the way they live.

James defines pure religion as reshaping one's life, character and behavior. In particular, pure religion entails being part of a community that reflects God's character and the kingdom he is about to bring. This kingdom is marked by two essential characteristics: pure and edifying speech, and practical expressions of care for the poor. This is the community of those who receive the implanted word and let it reshape their desires. The

---

28. See, for instance, McKnight, *James*, 167–68.
29. Cheung, *Genre*, 127; citing Borg, *Meeting Jesus*, 53.
30. Lockett, *Purity and Worldview*, 185.

motif of deception suggests that the κόσμος, because of its inability to transform, opposes pure speech and care for the poor and replaces these things with self-concern.

ΚΌΣΜΟΣ IN JAMES 2:5
General Import of James 2:1–13

The worldviews of faith and of the κόσμος clash at several levels, but the stress in this section falls on the definition of glory. This is indicated in the opening verse, in which James speaks of the "faith in our Lord Jesus Christ, the glorious one" (ἡ πίστις τοῦ κυρίου ἡμῶν Ἰησοῦ Χριστοῦ τῆς δόξης).[31] By placing the word "glory" (δόξα) in an emphatic position, James contrasts the manifestation of glory in Jesus Christ and in Greco-Roman society.[32] This opposition climaxes in vv. 5–6 where James accuses the community of despising the poor (ἀτιμάζω, v.6), whom God honors.

One should not think of the community as dealing with the poor more harshly than the rest of society would. Nothing in the reception of the poor depicted here exceeds the disregard generally manifested to the poor in the first century.[33] But the fact that the poor receive a similar treatment inside and outside the community scandalizes James: the church should be a different kind of community. James's tone and rhetoric in this section remain courteous, however. If he exposes the shortcomings of the community in a bold way, the tone shows that he assumes his audience had no bad intentions and simply overlooked the issue. "James hopes that, once shown the nature of partiality, the audience will refrain from it."[34]

This section thus aims at reshaping the community's core values. In the multicultural environment of Greco-Roman society, honor represented a challenge for any subculture, religious or not: "each group defined honorable and dishonorable conduct according to its own distinctive set of values

---

31. This translation takes the genitive phrase τῆς δόξης as epexegetical. For a similar reading, see Laws, *Commentary*, 95–96. The verse is notoriously difficult to translate and has produced a great deal of controversy. Some commentators propose smoothing the grammar by taking ἡμῶν Ἰησοῦ Χριστοῦ as a later interpolation. Allison (*James*, 382–84) summarizes the debate and the different readings that have been proposed.

32. See Assaël and Cuvillier, "Jacques 2.1," 145–51; Smit, "Exegesis and Proclamation," 62; Wachob, *Voice of Jesus*, 154–59.

33. Batten, "Degraded Poor," 74.

34. Watson, "James 2," 127.

and beliefs... Frequently, however, the values would clash."[35] As a result, a Christian definition of honor and glory had to be repeated and reinforced constantly. In order to do this, Jews and Christians adopted a few strategies, described by deSilva.

> First, group members need to be very clear about who constitutes their "court of reputation," that body of significant others whose "opinion" about what is honorable and shameful, and whose evaluation of the individual really matters. Their eyes need to be directed toward one another, toward their leaders, and, very frequently, toward beings beyond the visible sphere (for example, God or the honored members of the group who have moved to another realm after death) as they look for approval...
>
> A second critical strategy is, more or less, the mirror image of the first. Group members need to understand (and to articulate for one another) why the approval or disapproval of outsiders does not matter to the members of the group and why it is no reflection of the group members' true honor and worth.[36]

This is what James does here: he reframes the concept of honor, just as he reshaped the notion of purity in 1:26–27.

Exegesis of James 2:5

James writes:

ἀκούσατε, ἀδελφοί μου ἀγαπητοί·

οὐχ ὁ θεὸς ἐξελέξατο τοὺς πτωχοὺς τῷ κόσμῳ[37] πλουσίους ἐν πίστει καὶ κληρονόμους τῆς βασιλείας ἧς ἐπηγγείλατο τοῖς ἀγαπῶσιν αὐτόν;

---

35. deSilva, *Honor*, 37.
36. deSilva, *Honor*, 40.
37. A^c, C^2, P, Ψ, 5, 81, 307, 436, 442, 642, 1243, 1448, 1611, 1735, 1852, 2492 and the Byzantine manuscripts read τοῦ κόσμου while ℵ, A*, B, C*, 33, 1175, 1739 and 2344 read τῷ κόσμῳ. The earliest witnesses—ℵ (fourth century), A* (fifth century), B (fourth century), and C* (fifth century)—thus favor the latter reading, well attested both in Alexandrian and Western manuscripts. Apart from C2 (sixth century) and the uncertain date of the correction of A, the earliest attestations of τοῦ κόσμου comes from the ninth century (P, Ψ) and later. Timothy Johnson summarizes the matter quite nicely: "Both ἐν τῷ κόσμῳ and τοῦ κόσμου have poorer attestation, are longer, and are more easily explained as clarifications of τῷ κόσμῳ, which is shorter, harder, and better." Johnson, "Friendship," 212n38. See also Davids, *Epistle of James*, 112.

Listen, my beloved brothers:

Did not God choose the poor in the eyes of the world[38] to be rich in faith and heirs of the kingdom which he promised to those who love him?[39]

The expression τῷ κόσμῳ is interpreted here as a dative of reference, indicating that the state of poverty is an interpretation of reality *as viewed through the value system of the κόσμος*.[40] James does not view those who love God as poor; they are poor only in the eyes of the κόσμος. "In this passage, therefore, 'world' is a measure distinguishable from God's."[41] In the realm of "the world," the honor bestowed upon human beings is primarily grounded in their social status: "Honor is afforded those with wealth and power, while those without do not deserve any."[42]

In this passage, James witnesses to the fact that the church often adopts the world's way of seeing social realities, so that the error of "the world" is shared by Christians. As the extravagant vocabulary describing the rich man makes clear,[43] the community is spellbound by the visible display of riches and immediately honors the person (2:4).[44] In doing so, the

---

38. The dative phrase τῷ κόσμῳ has been the subject of much discussion. The precise grammatical tag does not affect the translation of the verse in any significant ways, however. For a summary of the grammatical options, see Frick, "Syntactical Note," 99–103.

39. The specific setting of these verses is debated, and the acts of partiality could either take place with visitors entering a worship service or at a time at which the community gathers to render judgment between a wealthy landowner and a poor tenant. For an argument for the latter position, see Ward, "Partiality," 87–97. Ward is followed by many scholars. For an evaluation on these two proposals, see Blomberg and Kamell, *James*, 110–11. The setting does not alter the overall meaning of the pericope or modify the tension between the value system of "the world" and the counter-cultural one championed by James. Therefore, the issue of the setting will not be further addressed here.

40. Agreeing with Johnson, *Letter of James*, 224; Davids, *Epistle of James*, 112; Moo, *James*, 107; Lockett, *Purity and Worldview*, 116; Dibelius, *James*, 138; Ropes, *Epistle of St. James*, 193.

41. Johnson, "Friendship," 212.

42. Hartin, *James*, 132. Similar statements can be found in classical and Hellenistic authors. Aristotle, for example, wrote that "A citizen who contributes nothing of value to the common stock is not held in honour, for the common property is given to those who benefit the community, and honour is a part fo the common property." Aristotle, *Eth. nic.* 8.14.3. See also Aristotle, *Rhet.* 2.5.7; Sir. 13:21–23.

43. See the description of the rich man (ἀνὴρ χρυσοδακτύλιος ἐν ἐσθῆτι λαμπρᾷ) and the verb used to express the gaze of everyone (ἐπιβλέπω).

44. Some commentators see the reaction of the community as a way to secure financial benefits from the wealthy visitor by taking him as a patron over the community. See

community aligns itself with the values of the κόσμος and, therefore, fails to perform its prophetic role of announcing God's perspective on people and on the world. James admonishes the community for its failure and invites it to regain a proper—i.e., eschatological—perspective.[45] This perspective will raise the community's awareness of the glory possessed by the poor and the arrogance of elevating oneself above the destitute, and enable the community to recover genuine love and mercy.

The Glory of the Poor

Although the community honors the rich, James considers wealth to be irrelevant to the realm of faith. It is, at best, disconnected from faith; more often, it possesses a corrupting influence. Wealth is fleeting, and the lives of those who attach too much importance to it will share its brevity (1:10–11; 4:14).

In contrast to the short-lived aspect of material wealth, the poor are described as chosen (ἐκλέγομαι) by God, rich in faith (πλουσίους ἐν πίστει), and heirs of the kingdom (κληρονόμος τῆς βασιλείας). Each of these expressions is important. First, the verb ἐκλέγομαι denotes covenant language, implying that God cares for the poor and that, in a particular way, they enjoy a special status before him. Hence, the strength of the relationship between God and the poor is stressed: "God chose the poor *for himself.*"[46] By choosing them, God grants them special honor.

Second, being rich in faith implies that the poor are "paradigmatic members" of the community: everyone else should learn from them.[47] Since faith (πίστις) in the Lord Jesus Christ (v. 1) defines the community, James presents the poor as perfectly attuned to the values the church should uphold.[48] "The poor, having nothing on which to rely except God, model the wholehearted trust in God and submission to his will that are

---

Vyhmeister, "Rich Man," 265–83; Kloppenborg Verbin, "Patronage Avoidance," 755–94; Batten, *Friendship*. While this could be a potential motivation of the community, James remains silent about it. Moreover, his argument aims at showing his audience where true wealth lies and what they should consequently value and honor. He gives no sign of rebuking them for trying to secure financial benefits by problematic means. His target is more encompassing than that.

45. The entire paragraph is to be read in light of Jas 2:12–13.

46. McKnight, *James*, 193n80.

47. Bauckham, *James*, 192.

48. On the topic of faith and the identity of the community, see Verseput, "Reworking the Puzzle," 97–115.

the authentic relationship of humanity to God (4:7, 10)."⁴⁹ This is further stressed when James identifies them with "those who love him [God]" (οἱ ἀγαπῶντες αὐτόν, 2:5). The expression is derived from Exod 20:6, a passage in which Moses describes God's character and faithfulness in the midst of the first commandment.⁵⁰ The full reference is to "those who love me and keep my commands" (οἱ ἀγαπῶντες με καὶ οἱ φυλάσσοντες τὰ προστάγματά μου), but the shortened form is already used in the later books of the OT as a way to refer to those who were remaining faithful to the covenant. It thus retained the full force of the expression found in Exodus (or in its parallels in Deut 5:10 and 7:9).⁵¹ James may also allude to the Shema (Deut 6:4–9) which brings together the command to love God and the command to keep his word.⁵² It is absolutely clear, therefore, that "loving God" describes not a feeling but a concrete way of life, so that the poor are described as those who are faithful to God's covenant.

Third, calling the poor "heirs of the kingdom" speaks about the eschatological reversal of status, when those who are neglected in the present order of things will be elevated and inherit the kingdom of God. The phrase "those who love him" plays an important role here as well. The repetition of the phrase in 1:12 and 2:5 creates a connection between those who receive the "crown of life" (ὁ στέφανος τῆς ζωῆς, 1:12) and the "heirs of the kingdom" (κληρονόμος τῆς βασιλείας, 2:5). This link implies that "the elect will become kings and rulers (crowned), and not only citizens of a kingdom."⁵³ In keeping with this metaphor, James qualifies the law as being "royal" in 2:8 (νόμος βασιλικός). He does not unpack what he means by this, but it most likely refers to the law given by the king. However, it may also indicate, albeit indirectly, that those who follow it are led to a royal status (just as the "law of freedom" in 2:12 is given to lead people to freedom).⁵⁴ The mention of inheriting the kingdom fits well in this context. In any case, by repeating the phrase "those who love him," James indicates that the poor, along with

---

49. Bauckham, *James*, 194.

50. The phrase "those who love me/God" appears first in Exod 20:6 and is repeated in Deut 5:10; 7:9.

51. See Judg 5:31; Neh 1:5; Dan 9:4; Ps 122:6; Tob 13:12, 14:7; Sir 1:10; *Pss. Sol.* 6:6, 14:1.

52. See McKnight, *James*, 113; Bauckham, *James*, 145; Hartin, *James*, 90.

53. Theissen, "Amour du prochain," 339.

54. For a discussion of different possible interpretations of "royal law," see Theissen, "Amour du prochain," 338–40; Cheung, *Genre*, 97–99.

all those who love God and follow his commands, will be elevated to a royal status in the coming kingdom.

In summary, James stresses the dignity and honor due to the poor both at present and in the future. They should be honored in the present time because God chose them as his special possession and because they are "rich in faith" (2:5). They will be even more honored when they receive their promised royal status in the coming kingdom. Because the κόσμος ignores the eschatological future that God has in store and the importance of faith, it is blind to the glory of the poor.

The Arrogance of Partiality

The audience's failure to recognize the glory of the poor suffices to indicate that they are not sharing God's perspective. Yet, James not only upholds the honor of the poor but also exposes the root of partiality and the reason it alienates the community from God.

Partiality presupposes an attitude of superiority from those who engage in it. The fictive scene in which the poor man is asked "to sit at the feet of my footstool" (κάθου ἐκεῖ ὑπὸ τὸ ὑποπόδιόν μου, v. 3) is an indictment of the hubris associated with partiality. The phrase is often read as emphatic, simply adding to the ridicule of the situation.[55] Some commentators see an allusion to Ps 110:1 (LXX 109:1), but nobody seems to have paid attention to the logical conclusion of such an echo.[56] If James alludes to Ps 110:1—a verse picturing God putting the Messiah's enemy under his feet—he implies much more than what is often thought. If there is an allusion to Ps 110:1, it does not stress the dishonor of the poor. Rather, it implies that the person who places himself above the poor usurps God's throne. To my knowledge, only Allison realizes this implication, even if only to discard it as improbable.[57]

---

55. Ward, "Partiality," 92; Vyhmeister, "Rich Man," 278; Kloppenborg Verbin, "Patronage Avoidance," 768.

56. Johnson, *Letter of James*, 223; McKnight, *James*, 188; Weaver, "Heart of the Law," 446. These scholars understand an allusion to Ps 110:1, but merely read it as a sign of humiliation.

57. Allison writes: "If one were to find an allusion to the oft-cited Ps 110.1, then one might think of the speaker as sufficiently pompous to speak ironically like God. But this seems far-fetched." Allison, *James*, 392n142. Yet, James does not present the speaker as "speak[ing] ironically like God." Rather, James tells the congregation that favoritism presupposes placing oneself on God's judgment seat.

However, there are strong indications that support the idea that James alludes to Ps 110:1 in order to warn his audience that despising the poor is equivalent to usurping God's throne. First, the word "footstool" (ὑποπόδιον) is a fairly rare noun.[58] Its occurrence here, in a rather unexpected context, should alert us to pay great attention. Second, the word "footstool" in the LXX *always* refers to God's footstool (representing the earth in Isa 66:1, the temple in Ps 99:5 and Lam 2:3) or to the footstool of his Messiah (representing his enemies, Ps 110:1). Since the NT authors (and the Apostolic Fathers) never use the word outside of OT quotations (of Isa 66:1; Ps 99:5; or Ps 110:1), it follows that the word is always used to refer to *God's* footstool in Scripture.[59] The later church fathers follow a similar pattern with very few exceptions.[60] Third, Ps 110 was well known in Christian circles, since it is one of the most frequently quoted text in the NT.[61] The textual variant in Jas 2:3 (adding τῶν ποδῶν as in LXX Ps 109:1), found *inter alia* in A, 33, and the Vg, is best explained as a textual corruption arising from familiarity with LXX Ps 109:1. Some scribes caught James's allusion and modified James's text—probably unintentionally—to make it correspond to their memory of the psalm. Finally, the idea that judging one's brother entails usurping God's prerogative—an idea Allison considers to be "far-fetched"—is precisely James's rebuke to those who revile (καταλαλέω) and judge (κρίνω) their neighbor in 4:11–12.[62] Given the language of judgment present in this pericope, it is no stretch to suppose that this is what James hints at. The invitation to "sit at the feet of my footstool" is not used for mere rhetorical emphasis, but as an implicit condemnation of arrogance. Practicing favoritism implies judging one's brother or sister and, therefore, robbing God of his throne.

58. The word ὑποπόδιον appears four times in the LXX (LXX Ps 98:5; 109:1; Isa 66:1; Lam 2:3), seven times in the NT, 3 times in the Apostolic Fathers (*1 Clem.* 36:5, *Barn.* 12:10, 16:2), once in Philo (*Conf.* 98), never in Josephus or the Greek apocrypha. These occurrences all speak about God's footstool.

59. Matthew 5:34-35 is not a proper quotation, but it certainly echoes Isa 66:1.

60. A quick look at an (English) anthology of the early church fathers reveals a similar pattern. In Schaff's ANF, the word "footstool" appears sixty-six times. Only five occurrences have nothing to do with God's footstool, one occurrence is a quote of Ps 99:5, and the other sixty are derived from either Ps 110:1 or Isa 66:1.

61. Psalm 110:1 is quoted in Matt 22:44; Mark 12:36; Luke 20:42; Acts 2:34; 1 Cor 15:25; Heb 1:13. It is echoed in Matt 26:64; Rom 8:34(?); Eph 1:20(?); Heb 1:3; 8:1; 10:12-13. Ps 110:4 is quoted in Heb 5:6; 7:17, 21, and echoed in Heb 6:20; 8:1.

62. Stulac writes: "In judging people, what we really want is to take God's place." Stulac, *James*, 154.

The same picture emerges in verses 6–7, in which James illustrates the logical outcome of holding to the worldview of the κόσμος. Those who hold to the value of "the world" (i.e., the rich) end up opposing Christ himself. It is not clear whether the oppression (καταδυναστεύω) and the dragging into court refer to the same reality or to different situations, nor whether the charges are religious or economic.[63] James 2:7 could be understood as a reference to religious persecution, but the wider context supports the interpretation of a trial on an economic basis. In that case, "this legal action [would be] over such issues as debts, rents, wages, and pledges."[64] Whatever prompted the oppression, the rich misuse their power in abusing people belonging to the community. For James, oppressing the poor is tantamount to insulting God himself. The rich are not only charged with wickedness but with blasphemy: they violate the power and the majesty of God.

In short, favoritism is denounced as opposing the eschatological reversal God will bring about and, therefore, God's rule itself. Favoritism ignores God's choice of the poor (2:5), and those who practice it affirm boundaries that ought to disappear in God's kingdom—and so also in the church. In negating God's values, favoritism resists God's rule and replaces it with the standards of judgment belonging to "the world." Hence, those who associate with the κόσμος are not only blind to eschatological realities, they also oppose God's kingdom by trying to suppress and usurp his rule.

ΚΌΣΜΟΣ IN JAMES 3:6

Translation Issues

καὶ ἡ γλῶσσα πῦρ ὁ κόσμος τῆς ἀδικίας ἡ γλῶσσα καθίσταται ἐν τοῖς μέλεσιν ἡμῶν ἡ σπιλοῦσα ὅλον τὸ σῶμα καὶ φλογίζουσα τὸν τροχὸν τῆς γενέσεως καὶ φλογιζομένη ὑπὸ τῆς γεέννης.[65]

---

63. See discussion in Allison, *James*, 399.

64. Maynard-Reid, *Poverty*, 63–64.

65. The sentence is notoriously difficult to translate, and two emendations have been proposed. Dibelius thought that "the words from ὁ κόσμος through ἡμῶν must constitute a gloss." James B. Adamson proposed adding he word ὕλη (wood) after ἀδικίας. The sentence would then explain further the image of fire at the end of v.5: "The tongue is a fire, the evil world wood." This is the reading of the Peshitta. Richard Bauckham follows Adamson on this. Dibelius, *James*, 195; Adamson, *Epistle of James*, 158–59; Bauckham, "Tongue," 119n1; cf. Bauckham, *James*, 54.

The tongue also [is] a fire; the tongue—which defiles the whole body and sets the course of [our] life⁶⁶ on fire and is [itself] set on fire by [the fire of] Gehenna—appoints itself [as] the unrighteous world among our members.⁶⁷

The occurrence of κόσμος in Jas 3:6 is the most difficult to assess. For one thing, the expression ὁ κόσμος τῆς ἀδικίας is ambiguous and could be construed in at least two ways.⁶⁸ The Vulgate translates the phase as "the totality of iniquity" (*universitas iniquitatis*), a reading that finds a parallel in LXX Prov 17:6 (ὅλος ὁ κόσμος τῶν χρημάτων). If such a reading is accepted, then this occurrence of κόσμος stands apart and does not help us to further develop the concept described by κόσμος in James's letter. Although it enjoyed some popularity among ancient commentators, few modern scholar defend this option.⁶⁹ The phrase is best translated as "the world of unrighteousness" or "the unrighteous world." The benefit of this reading is twofold. First, the syntax would be easy to account for through an appeal to Hebrew or Aramaic background.⁷⁰ Second, it gives this occurrence of the word κόσμος a meaning similar to the one it carries in its other four occurrences in James. Most commentators therefore prefer this reading.⁷¹

Understanding the grammar of the verse also proves difficult. The sentence is so fraught with grammatical difficulties that Dibelius claims "there are few verses in the New Testament which suggest the hypothesis of a textual corruption as much as this one does."⁷² Indeed, the string of nominative expressions linked with a single verb (καθίστημι) opens up many

---

66. On the meaning and background of the expression ὁ τροχός τῆς γενέσεως, see Dibelius (*James*, 195–98), who argues that James "is signifying little more than 'life.'" The value given to the phrase does not affect the exegesis here and will not be discussed.

67. For a similar rendering, see Laws, *Commentary*, 148–50; Davids, *Epistle of James*, 142.

68. A third option, reading κόσμος as meaning adornment (cf. 1 Pet 3:3), exists. In this reading, the tongue makes unrighteousness appealing. Because it assumes a rare meaning of κόσμος and does not fit the context very well, this view is rarely defended. For a defense of it, see Chaine, *L'Épitre de Saint Jacques*, 81; Cambe, "Isidore de Péluse," 387–411.

69. Bede, *Seven Catholic Epistles*, 39; Calvin, *Catholic Epistles*, 320. For a list of other writers who defend this option, see Mayor, *James*, 110.

70. Allison, *James*, 536.

71. See Dibelius, *James*, 194; Laws, *Commentary*, 150; Moo, *Letter of James*, 129; McKnight, *James*, 283; Davids, *Epistle of James*, 142; Allison, *James*, 536; Adam, *James*, 65; McCartney, *James*, 187.

72. Dibelius, *James*, 194.

possibilities in the way the nouns relate to one another. The translation proposed above reads "the world of unrighteousness" (ὁ κόσμος τῆς ἀδικίας) as an articular predicate to the verb "appoints itself" (καθίστημι; parsed as a middle voice rather than as a passive).[73]

Meaning of the Verse

The overall theme of this section (3:1–12) stresses the discrepancy between the size of the tongue and the magnitude of its effects (3:5), using both with positive (3:3–4) and negative images (3:6–8).[74] For James, controlling the tongue is essential: it either enables a person to guide "the whole body" (ὅλον τὸ σῶμα, 3:2) or it defiles "the whole body" (ὅλον τὸ σῶμα, 3:6). In any case, the tongue's effects are all-encompassing. Jewish wisdom tradition also stresses the power of the tongue for life or for death (see Prov 18:21), but James focuses on the destructive power of the tongue, as the images of fire (3:6) and poison (3:8) make clear. Whenever the tongue is not controlled (3:2), it wreaks havoc in the person.

If the translation proposed above is correct, this verse makes a crucial contribution to our analysis of James's understanding of κόσμος. "The unrighteous world" is not alien to the Christian, but has a seat within him or her. James does not conceive of evil as only external to the person. "The world" cannot be escaped. None can flee from it; it burns within the body.[75] Since the tongue resists being tamed by human beings (v. 8), it sounds as if James has pronounced the ineluctable doom of humankind.

The idea that the κόσμος is rooted in human beings has two major consequences. The first is not spelled out by James but is a logical outcome: if evil is rooted in human beings rather than in some corrupt organization of society, it follows that the social evils described by James are inescapable. According to James, the ultimate reason for the tribulations of the poor is not a corrupt system or a bad organization of society, but the presence of a

---

73. Contra McKnight who prefers the passive (*James*, 283). The middle is defended by Laws who stresses its reflexive force. See Laws, *Commentary*, 149; Moo, *James*, 158. The other option would be to read the expression as an apposition to the first clause: "the tongue [is] a fire, namely the world of unrighteousness." It is difficult, however, to make sense of this reading.

74. Following Dibelius (*James*, 192); *contra* Bertram ("Ὁρμή," 471), who reads these images negatively. Bertram sees people being powerless against the whims of the tongue.

75. It should be mentioned in passing that this verse provides clear evidence that James does not advocate for a sectarian separation from society. A community that would hide from society would still bring the world with itself.

corrupt system of values rooted in the human heart. Corrupt systems may exist and lead to oppression, but these are symptoms of a deeper problem. This is not to say that one should not oppose these oppressive systems: James does. He does not seem to assume, however, that social evils can be eradicated apart from uprooting evil from the human heart.[76]

Second, left on its own, humanity has not the slightest hope of escaping its predicament. The tongue not only inflames the present life (ὁ τροχός τῆς γενέσεως), it is also "set on fire by Gehenna" (φλογιζομένη ὑπὸ τῆς γεέννης). The mention of Gehenna is a direct reference to eschatological judgment. Although many commentators take Gehenna—seen as the abode of Satan—as being the *source* of evil,[77] Bauckham demonstrated the impossibility of this reading.[78] In Jewish tradition, Gehenna's angels "are servants of God, executing God's judgment on sin. . . [T]he fire of Gehenna is always a means or an image of God's judgment."[79] Moreover, Bauckham argues that punishment as fire is an example of the "eschatological *ius talionis*."[80] Because the tongue inflames human passions—and, by doing so, brings destruction in human communities—it will be punished by fire. The way people use their tongue, therefore, has eternal significance.

James is not entirely pessimistic, however. The hope he proposes consists in welcoming God's wisdom. The second part of Jas 3 (vv. 13–18)—and especially the qualities of the "wisdom from above" listed in verse 17—corresponds to all the problems raised in the first (3:1–12). Wisdom is pure (ἁγνός), as opposed to the defiling influence (σπιλόω, v. 6) of the tongue. It is "peaceable" and "gentle" (εἰρηνικός, ἐπιεικής) in contrast to the "restless evil" (ἀκατάστατος κακός, v. 8) of the tongue. It is "full of mercy" (μεστὸς ἐλέους) rather than "full of deadly poison" (μεστὸς ἰοῦ θανατηφόρου, v. 8). It is "obedient" (εὐπειθής), unlike the tongue that "no one is able to tame" (οὐδεὶς δαμάσαι δύναται, v. 8). Wisdom bears only "good fruits" (καρπός ἀγαθός), in contrast to the picture of mixed fruits or the spring that produces fresh and salty water (vv. 10–12). It does not produce division (ἀδιάκριτος) and it is not hypocritical (ἀνυπόκριτος), unlike those who bless God and curse

---

76. The same idea is implicit in Jas 1:21.

77. See for instance Baker, who sees Gehenna as a "euphemism for Satan." Moo and Laws also cite this option as one possibility. Baker, *Personal Speech-Ethics*, 77; Moo, *James*, 130; Laws, *James*, 152.

78. Bauckham, "Tongue," 119–31.

79. Bauckham, "Tongue," 120.

80. Bauckham, "Tongue," 123.

people (v. 9).⁸¹ Finally, and most importantly, wisdom produces a "harvest of righteousness" (καρπὸς δὲ δικαιοσύνης, v. 18) instead of the destruction by fire promised to those who do not control their tongue. The reception of wisdom answers all the problems caused by evil speech.

As James stated earlier, this wisdom is a gift of God, generously offered to whoever asks in faith (1:5–6). Because wisdom turns people away from these evils and prepares a "harvest of righteousness," there is no doubt that it can be equated with "the word of truth" that gives birth to people in the community (1:18) and "has the power to save the soul" (1:21).⁸²

James 3:6 teaches us that the κόσμος resides within every human being, bringing destruction and division among people. Moreover, the evil stemming from "the world" is irresistible—or, in James's words, impossible to tame. Humanity's only hope is to receive, through prayer, the wisdom from above, the only antidote to the deadly poison of the tongue.

JAMES 3:15 AND THE EARTHLY WISDOM

In the section we just looked at, James not only describes the "wisdom from above," he also contrasts it with the pseudo-wisdom of "the world." Even though James never uses the term κόσμος in this section, the opposition between the two "wisdoms" makes the link between "the world" and "earthly wisdom" (ἐπίγειος) clear enough. Moreover, these few verses serve as a transition between James's comments on pure speech (3:1–12) and his discussion about envy (4:1–10), in which he articulates the opposition between God and "the world."

James sheds light on the sources of pseudo-wisdom by describing it as "earthly, unspiritual, demonic" (ἐπίγειος, ψυχικός, δαιμονιώδης). One can first observe that James holds to a clear moral dualism. No middle ground exists. Everything is tracked back to its ultimate source: God or demons.⁸³ The adjective "earthly" (ἐπίγειος), in a context where it is contrasted with what comes "from above," indicates that the pseudo-wisdom's insights

---

81. Three other textual links strengthen the connections between these two sections. The word "bitter" (πικρός) in v. 11 ("salted water") is echoed in v. 14 ("bitter jealousy"), and the adjective "restless" (ἀκατάστατος) in v. 8 anticipates the cognate noun, "disorder" (ἀκαταστασία), in v. 16. Boasting against the truth (καυχάομαι, v. 14) also echoes the tongue's boasting (αὐχέω, v. 6).

82. Hartin argues for the same chain of connections. See Hartin, *Spirituality of Perfection*, 77.

83. On moral dualism, see also McKnight, *James*, 306.

are limited to earthly life, ignoring God's transcendence. In other words, it is not open to receive anything from God. The term ψυχικός (literally: "pertaining to the soul," translated here by "unspiritual") bears a similar connotation. As in most Christian literature, it is used as an antonym to πνευματικός ("spiritual"), and reinforces the opposition between earthly wisdom and wisdom from above.[84] Finally, "demonic" (δαιμονιώδης) leaves the reader in no doubt about James's perspective. In his view, the values of the earthly realm are inspired by the devil himself. Such a view is coherent within typical Jewish cosmology and anticipates Jas 4:4.[85]

Second, the language of "above" and "below" evokes a spatial perspective. The contrast is not between the present life and the life to come—as in many other early Christian writings—but between the heaven and the earth.[86] Whereas eschatological language enables an author to stress the sense of hope, speaking of a "wisdom from above" and an "earthly wisdom" emphasizes instead that two "worlds" coexist in parallel—that the heavenly realm is also a present reality. Here, the reader is asked to align him- or herself with the heavenly reality, and turn it into a *present* reality in his or her own situation. Although James displays a clear eschatological hope at many points in the epistle, here he does not direct attention to the hope of future restoration, but to God's transcendence as the inspiration to live the present life differently. "Attention is directed, not to past or future, but to the ongoing present as the moment of action and decision."[87]

Finally, the irreconcilable division between the two kinds of wisdom and their respective origins is manifested by their outcomes. James does not attack human wisdom *per se*. He targets the "anti-wisdom" that manifests itself through "jealousy" (ζῆλος, 3:14, 16) and "selfish ambition" (ἐριθεία, 3:14, 16).[88] By contrast, the wisdom from above—a euphemistic reference to wisdom coming from God himself—is manifested by purity and a peaceful attitude (cf. the qualities mentioned in the previous section). Ultimately, anyone who is moved by jealousy or ambition, whether outside or within the church, is inspired by demonic forces and, thus, plays Satan's game.

---

84. The words occur in the NT in 1 Cor 2:15; 15:44, 46; Jude 19, each time as a contrast to what is spiritual. See Silva, "Ψυχή κτλ.," 4:731–32.

85. See Bauckham, "Tongue," 120.

86. See, for instance, Gal 1:4; Rom 8:18; 12:2; 1 Cor 1:26; 2:6–7; 2 Cor 4:18; 1 John 2:17. For temporal dualism in Judaism, see *1 En.* 71:15; *4 Ezra* 7:43, 50; 8:1.

87. Elliott, "Holiness-Wholeness," 77.

88. The term "anti-wisdom" is borrowed from Hartin, *Spirituality of Perfection*, 73.

The wisdom from above thus makes it possible for the community to build itself on a solid basis, whereas the wisdom from the earth undermines the foundation of the community by fostering competition, jealousy and strife.

ΚΌΣΜΟΣ IN JAMES 4:4

The word κόσμος appears for the last time in Jas 4:4, in the context of a call to repentance. James 4:1–6 exposes the problem and convicts the culprits, while 4:7–10 invites them to repent by humbling themselves in order to be, eventually, elevated by God (4:10). The *inclusio* built around the verb "to oppose" (ἀντιτάσσω, in 4:6 and 5:6) also suggests that James employs the contrast between God raising the humble and opposing the proud as a thematic statement.[89] James 4:7–10 thus invites the readers to humble themselves, while the three scenes presented in 4:11–5:6 exemplify arrogant behaviors that they should avoid. The change of tone in these verses is especially striking.

> The familial relationship that has to this point emphatically structured the author-audience relationship in the letter now begins to recede into the background. Indeed, by 4.4 the usual framing of the audience as "brothers" has been fully eclipsed by convicting, distancing addresses to them as "adulterers" (4.4), "sinners" (4.8) and δίψυχοι (4.8; cf. 1.6–8).[90]

In many ways, this section brings James's letter to a climactic tension or, to borrow William Varner's term, a "zone of turbulence."[91]

Preliminary Observations on the Targeted Audience

Before discussing the meaning of the κόσμος in this passage, one needs to identify James's target audience in these verses. One possible approach—adopted, for instance, by Scot McKnight—would be to assume that "James has not changed the focus of his attention since 3:1; he is concerned with teachers, their tongues, and the communal destructiveness they are

---

89. See Schökel, "James 5:2 [sic]," 73–76.
90. Jackson-McCabe, "Enduring Temptation," 173–74.
91. Varner, "Main Theme," 128.

generating."⁹² Whether Jas 4:1–10 is addressed to teachers only or to every believer impacts the weight of the passage and needs to be clarified.

McKnight's proposal is promising. First, the charge against strife in 4:1–3 could easily flow from Jas 3:17–18, which emphasizes the bond of peace built by those who live according to the wisdom from above. In this reading, James condemns the vices that render that peace impossible. Multiple other connections between 3:13–18 and 4:1–10 can be pointed out, so that many scholars take 3:13–4:10 as a single unity.⁹³ A second argument comes from the text James seems to be quoting in verse 5.⁹⁴ The passage is notoriously difficult to translate,⁹⁵ but it almost certainly functions as an indictment of envy (φθόνος).⁹⁶ Bauckham and Allison offer convincing arguments that James is here citing the lost book of Eldad and Modad.⁹⁷ If they are right, James points to a lost text that develops Moses' answer to Joshua when he manifests jealousy towards two people who prophecy in the camp (cf. Num 11:26–29). "Just as Moses rebuked the jealous Joshua, who protested the grace unexpectedly given to Eldad and Modad, so James rebukes those in the synagogue who, out of envy and selfish desire, are cursing, disputing, slandering, and judging others."⁹⁸ This reading would then reinforce the idea that the passage is especially addressed to spiritual leaders who envy others for their gifts or prominent positions. Finally, McKnight's proposal is in line with the use of φθόνος, since this word was often

---

92. McKnight, *James*, 320.

93. On ties between 3:13–18 and 4:1–10, one could mention the similar opposition between the two types of wisdom (from above or from below) and the opposition between God and the world; the idea that the wisdom from below is demonic (δαιμονιώδης, 3:15) while "the world" remains subject to the devil (διάβολος, 4:8); the lexical parallels between pure wisdom (ἁγνός, 3:17) and the call to purify one's heart (ἁγνίζω, 4:8), etc. For a fuller list, see Martin, *James*, 142. Authors adopting this position include Martin, *James*, 141–44; Johnson, "James 3:13–4:10," 327–47; Hartin, *James*, 203–17; Painter and deSilva, *James and Jude*, 183; Jackson-McCabe, "Enduring Temptation."

94. The verse runs as follows in Greek: "Ἢ δοκεῖτε ὅτι κενῶς ἡ γραφὴ λέγει· πρὸς φθόνον ἐπιποθεῖ τὸ πνεῦμα ὃ κατῴκισεν ἐν ἡμῖν.

95. Allison references eighteen different interpretations of this verse and adds that most of these could be turned into questions. There is no need to discuss the difficulties of the verse in detail here. See Allison, *James*, 613–14.

96. In Scripture, as in pagan literature, φθόνος (envy) always bears a pejorative connotation. For a list of references, see Allison, *James*, 611n125.

97. See Bauckham, "Spirit of God," 270–81; Allison, "Eldad and Modad," 99–131.

98. Allison, *James*, 622.

"defined as sadness occasioned by the thought of another's good."[99] The idea of being envious of the gift of other teachers makes sense of verse 3, in which those who envy are presented as asking God for what they desire, albeit with wrong motives. It is easier to imagine teachers praying for the gift of insight in Scripture or rhetorical skill than to imagine a first-century Christian earnestly praying for a multiplication of his or her wealth.[100] We therefore have good reasons to assume that James is primarily targeting some spiritual leaders.

At the same time, one should recognize that James never mentions such leaders explicitly. The theme of pure speech itself seems to extend beyond teachers. The general comments on the tongue in chapter 3 indicate that the concrete warning not to become teachers (3:1) has given way to more general concerns about speech in the community. To be sure, proper speech is especially important for teachers (3:1), but it also concerns the rest of the community. Laws observes that already in 3:13 "there is no indication that the description of wisdom is addressed especially to the would-be teachers of iii. 1 . . . According to i. 5, it is open to anyone to ask for wisdom."[101] This is especially true since receiving God's wisdom, the "wisdom from above," is necessary in order to be faithful to God, to develop faith to its perfect status. Leaders may need to develop them to a particularly high degree, but these qualities are essential to the faithful life as James describes it. Therefore, even though teachers are probably those most directly rebuked, it is safe to posit a universal application for Jas 4:1–10.

It is also clear from the whole passage that James rebukes only believers, not people outside of the community. The image of adultery presupposes a covenant relationship, and the assumption that readers are already aware of the enmity between the κόσμος and God implies they have been taught the basics of faith already.[102] The image of double-mindedness (4:8) also makes sense only if those who desire to please the κόσμος are believers.

---

99. Spicq, "Φθόνος," 435. See note 5 for references.

100. The NT provides a few examples of people who plan to use religion as a source of financial gain, all of whom are condemned for it (see, for instance, John 12:6; Luke 16:14; Acts 8:20). Christian writers often warned their audiences against people who were trying to turn faith into a source of income (see 1 Tim 6:5–10; Titus 1:11; 2 Pet 2:3; Jude 11; *Did.* 11:3–12). Since James encourages his readers to ask in prayer what they long for, it seems very unlikely that desire for money is what he has in view here.

101. Laws, *Commentary*, 158–59.

102. Johnson asks how the readers were supposed to know this and proposes a common Christian tradition "whose origin we no longer know." Johnson, "Friendship," 209.

New Elements about Κόσμος in James 4:4

In the first three verses of this chapter, James chastises his readers for allowing unchecked desires to fester and provoke feuds. This, for James, amounts to aligning oneself with "the world," and thus to spiritual adultery:

Μοιχαλίδες,[103] οὐκ οἴδατε ὅτι ἡ φιλία τοῦ κόσμου ἔχθρα τοῦ θεοῦ ἐστιν;
ὃς ἐὰν οὖν βουληθῇ φίλος εἶναι τοῦ κόσμου, ἐχθρὸς τοῦ θεοῦ καθίσταται.[104]

> Adulteresses! Do you not know that friendship with the world is enmity with God?
> Therefore, whoever wants to be a friend of the world appoints himself as God's enemy.

This pericope stresses a few crucial elements of James's understanding of the κόσμος. First, James equates "the world" with a false god. James's address ("adulteresses!") takes its inspiration from the OT prophets who used the same image to warn Israel against idolatry (cf. esp. Hos 3:1; see also Mal 3:5; Ezek 23:35). The theme of idolatry reinforces the idea that aligning oneself with the κόσμος leads to blindness and deception (see the section on Jas 1:26–27 above). In Scripture, idolatry is often described as leading to spiritual blindness.[105] Speaking of idolatry also highlights the fact that "friendship with the world" is a matter of life and death. James is not offering advice pertaining to spiritual maturity. Rather, James's call to repentance is a solemn warning that those who seek "friendship with the world" are actually courting death. The urgency of James's tone comes from his conviction that those who take that path are stepping outside the boundaries of the covenant and choosing death.

In line with the identification of the κόσμος as an idol, the language of "friendship with the world" in 4:4 implies that "the world" is personified. For the first time, it is presented as an entity that one can love and that is

---

Many point to Matt 6:24, Jesus' saying that one cannot serve God and Mammon. See Hartin, *Spirituality of Perfection*, 107–08; Garland, "Severe Trials," 389; Konradt, "Love Command," 280; Kloppenborg, "Q, Thomas, and James," 119.

103. A number of manuscripts have μοιχοὶ καὶ μοιχαλίδες instead. The earliest MSS ($\mathfrak{P}^{100}$, ℵ*, A, B) all have the feminine alone. The variant is commonly regarded as an attempt to smooth the language of James addressing his audience with a feminine noun. This, however, is to miss the allusion to the OT prophets, who describe idolatrous Israel as an unfaithful wife.

104. Two other variants exist, but do not influence the interpretation of the verse and need not be discussed here.

105. See Beale, *We Become*, 41–49.

able to respond to such love. In contrast to 1:27 and 2:5, here the κόσμος is presented as more than a value system: it stands for a personified reality. James does not provide much information on what he means by this, but it seems that the κόσμος is seen as a collective person. As human society is bound together in the pursuit of wealth and status rather than God's righteousness, humanity becomes a personified agent with a single will that stands in opposition to God.[106] This motif is no doubt connected with the fact that James equates the κόσμος with an idol. The human attitude towards wealth and status turns the κόσμος into an idol since it receives the kind of devotion and interest that is appropriately directed to God alone.[107] This also explains the close connection James draws between "the world" and the devil (διάβολος, 4:7).

It follows that "friendship with the world" is simply a euphemism to speak about "friendship with the devil" (cf. 4:7). The opposition between God and the κόσμος is now complete. No option exists besides following God or following the κόσμος. This is clearly set out in verse 4, but the whole passage underlines the idea, especially in James's playful choice of words in 4:6–7. Assonances and compounds sharpen the opposition: a person can either submit to God (ὑποτάσσω, 4:7), or God will oppose (ἀντιτάσσω, 4:6) that person; either Satan is resisted (ἀνθίστημι), or the believer will be resisted (ἀντιτάσσω) by God. In other words, "the world" is not one false god among others, but rather encompasses everything that sets itself against God and his law. Davids's proposition that "the world stands for human culture, mores, and structures, which are organized without God" and, therefore, opposed to him, is perfectly appropriate here.[108] The κόσμος stands for more than the value system opposed to the values of God's kingdom (as in 1:27 and 2:5); it is also the human matrix built on that worldview (in 4:4). Those who build their lives on these values are thus doubly guilty:

---

106. This depiction of "the world" is most often found in Johannine writings. See Sasse, "Κοσμέω κτλ.," 3:889–95.

107. The same line of thought seems to be in the background of Col 3:5 and adds a further argument to those who think that Matt 6:24—which considers money (Mammon) to be an idol—stands at the background of Jas 4:4.

108. Davids, *James*, 100. See also Hiebert, *Epistle of James*, 250–51. Allison takes the verse to mean that "the world—not just human society—is no longer God's world" (*James*, 609). Apart from many parallels in Jewish texts, he does not provide arguments for giving "the world" such a universal scope.

they are exposed as idolaters and, as participants in a corrupt system, they are condemned as instruments of oppression.[109]

Second, James confirms what was hinted at in 3:15. Since resisting the devil (διάβολος, 4:7) is necessary to break one's "friendship with the world," it follows that the devil and the κόσμος are intimately related. The devil is thus revealed as the hidden power promoting and sustaining the perverted value system of the κόσμος.

The divisive nature of the κόσμος is also emphasized. It creates division both in the community and in the human heart. James asks his audience two rhetorical questions in verse 1. The first question—"where do the fights and quarrels among you come from?"—invites the reader to think about the source of the quarrels between people.[110] The second provides the answer: "Is it not from your pleasures which wage war within you [lit: in your members]?"[111] Whereas 3:6 introduced the tongue as the organ through which "the world" gets a foothold in the human person, this passage presents *pleasures* (ἡδονή, vv. 1, 3) and *desires* (see the verbs ἐπιθυμέω and ζηλόω in v. 2) as other means of influence. Desires and pleasures work against single-mindedness (4:8). For James, divisions in the social body stem from divided hearts. When pleasures are given freedom to develop, the wisdom from above cannot produce its fruit of peace (3:17–18).[112]

Fourth, the κόσμος stands for a way of death. At first sight, the mention of murder (φονεύω, v. 2) intrigues.[113] It seems unlikely that James describes

109. The lack of response to prayer in Jas 4:3 can already be taken as a sign of God's opposition and, as Moo (*James*, 148) points out, "enmity with God" (ἔχθρα τοῦ θεοῦ) means "not only a hostility of the believer towards God, but of God towards the believer." Moreover, the theme of God's opposition reappears in 5:6 ("Does [God] not resist you?" οὐκ ἀντιτάσσεται ὑμῖν; read as a rhetorical question with God as the implied subject), where God is said to oppose the rich who exploit their hired workers. For a defense of this reading of 5:6, see Schökel, "James 5:2 [sic]"; Johnson, *Letter of James*, 305.

110. Πόθεν πόλεμοι καὶ πόθεν μάχαι ἐν ὑμῖν; The preposition ἐν should be understood as quarrels among different people from the congregation, as do virtually all translations.

111. Οὐκ ἐντεῦθεν, ἐκ τῶν ἡδονῶν ὑμῶν τῶν στρατευομένων ἐν τοῖς μέλεσιν ὑμῶν; In this reading, "in your members" (ἐν τοῖς μέλεσιν ὑμῶν) is interpreted as tensions within each person rather than between different members of the community. The majority of interpreters read the verse this way. See Adamson, *Epistle of James*, 166; Martin, *James*, 145; Davids, *Epistle of James*, 157; Allison, *James*, 600. For a defense of the other position, see McKnight, *James*, 324.

112. On the link between Jas 4:1–3 and what precedes it, see Hartin, *Spirituality of Perfection*, 75.

113. The charge does not seem to fit the context very well. An attempt to smooth the text has been offered by Erasmus, who proposed, despite the lack of textual evidence,

actual killing; rather, "murder" functions rhetorically as an emphatic depiction of anger or hate—i.e., the outcome of following one's desires rather than the law of freedom.[114] James then likely follows Jesus's lead in equating anger stemming from frustrated desires with murder.[115] Dietrich Bonhoeffer captures this idea powerfully: "Those who allow their own desire to become their god, must inevitably hate other human beings who stand in their way and impede their designs."[116] In the final analysis, however, whether or not James has actual murder in mind is irrelevant. His point is clear: brooding desires lead to violence—perpetrated or hidden, verbal or physical. In both cases, the κόσμος leads to death.

Finally, the selfish nature of the κόσμος comes out more clearly than before. If Jas 2 rebukes those who align with "the world" for fear of giving the little they have or from a lack of courage to stand against the dominant culture, this passage presents people envying the success of others to the point of destroying the peace of the community. Like many philosophers before him, James points to the destructive power of the selfish desires that comes from envy. If the reading proposed above is correct, envious teachers would rather see an end to the fruitful ministry of others—a desire symbolized by the verb φονεύω—rather than be forced to witness the fact that others are more successful or gifted than themselves.[117] Envy is an ultimate evil because it causes one not only to seek to gain or keep a good for oneself, but also to prefer the destruction in others of the good one lacks for oneself.

EXCURSUS: THE ΚΌΣΜΟΣ AND THE CREATED REALM

We saw that the κόσμος is primarily a value system, a worldview closed in on itself and sustained by the demonic powers that give it its power. Moreover, humanity by and large supports and perpetuates that worldview because it has a foothold in human beings through their desires. In that definition, the earth—or the created realm—is not part of the κόσμος and

---

to emend the text from φονεύετε to φθονεῖτε. He is followed, among others by Calvin, *Catholic Epistles*; Adamson, *Epistle of James*, 168; Allison, *James*, 602.

114. *Pace* Townsend, "Zealotry," 211–13; Martin, *James*, 146; McKnight, *James*, 326.

115. Cf. Matt 5:21–22. Moo, for example, also defends this line of thought (*James*, 146).

116. Dietrich Bonhoeffer, quoted in Allison, *James*, 601.

117. For a parallel to this idea, see also *T. Sim.* 3:3. Other examples are given in Spicq, "Φθόνος."

does not participate in that corruption. Yet it is not uncommon to read in commentaries statements claiming that "the world—not just human society—is no longer God's world."[118] Painter and deSilva, writing about the fact that Jas 3:15 equates earthly wisdom with demonic wisdom, write that "God's earth becomes the godless world."[119] Are we restricting the meaning of the κόσμος too much by limiting it to a worldview?

In order to answer that question satisfactorily, an important distinction—one that is unfortunately not stressed frequently enough—needs to be made.[120] On the one hand, James does not include the earth in his definition of the κόσμος. On the other hand, the earth (γῆ) *is* the realm in which the κόσμος manifests itself.

Let us first develop the idea that the created order is *not* part of the κόσμος. We can begin with the first occurrence of the word, in Jas 1:27. As we have seen, the κόσμος is here defined as a polluting (σπιλόω) influence to avoid. Since κόσμος is not further defined, reading the word as meaning either "the sum total of everything here and now" or "planet earth as a place of inhabitation" is simply impossible.[121] This would imply a sort of otherworldly spirituality in which matter itself should be escaped. Such an otherworldly spirituality would contradict not only the rest of the epistle, but also all known streams of Judaism. Such a belief would be fully gnostic. Once one tries to see if these definitions of "the world" could fit the others verses, one quickly recognizes that it simply does not work.

The phrases of Allison and deSilva quoted above should therefore be understood as simply saying that the earth—because it is the place in which human beings live—has become the sad stage on which the polluting effect of the κόσμος is visible. The earth is not in itself a corrupting influence, but the corruption of human behavior happens on the earth.[122] To that extent, it makes sense to speak of the earth as not being under God's rule.

However, one should note that whereas the earth (γῆ) is the place where human beings are corrupted by the κόσμος, it is *also* the locus of

118. Allison, *James*, 609.

119. Painter and deSilva, *James and Jude*, 183.

120. We are not discussing here whether human society as such has a corrupting influence and needs to be held at a distance—the sectarian tendency. This will be discussed in the next chapter. We are speaking here of the idea that the material realm itself has a polluting influence.

121. BDAG, s.v. κόσμος, §3 and §5 respectively.

122. This is carefully explored in Lockett, "God and 'the World,'" 144–56. Bauckham ("Tongue," 121) agrees.

God's redemption. As we will see in Chapter 4, below, the rain watering the earth functions in Jas 5:7 and 5:18 as a symbol of hope for God's restoration *of the earth*.[123] Moreover, Jas 3:9—where the image of God in human beings still provides the ground for human dignity—offers a clear basis on which to argue that James does not hold to a complete corruption of humankind and so, *a fortiori*, of the created order. Although it may be in a poor state, God's creation is nonetheless redeemable.

Before closing this section, a final comment is in order. Sentences similar to the quotes of Allison and deSilva abound in commentaries and articles on James. Though their rhetorical power is undeniable, such formulations are unfortunate because they can create a confusion in terms, suggesting a form of escapism alien to James's intention.[124] If such an escapism rarely surfaces in scholarly work, it is not infrequent in popular Christianity. Consequently, biblical scholars would do a great service to lay Christians by avoiding possible misunderstanding on these issues so as not to encourage an escapist view of salvation that they do not themselves adhere to. David Wilkinson's word of caution concerning escapist eschatology is valid here as well: "It may not be theological mainstream, but the theological mainstream must engage with it not least to help the large number of evangelical Christians to better understand the nature of creation and new creation."[125]

CONCLUSION

A consistent picture emerges from the various texts in which James speaks of "the world." First and foremost, the κόσμος depicts a *set of values* diametrically opposed to those of God's kingdom. It is defined as an "earthly" worldview—that is, a worldview that ignores heavenly realities. The κόσμος does not take into account the possibility of God's intervention, either positively (providing the wisdom from above) or negatively (bringing

---

123. One could also argue that taking an illustration from the created order as a rebuke for duplicity in Jas 3:10–12 points to the idea that nature opposes human double-mindedness. Such an argument is weakened, however, by the fact that James also employs nature as a source of images of double-mindedness (waves of the sea in 1:6), transience (flower of grass in 1:10; mist in 4:14), or fickleness (the astronomical vocabulary in 1:17 contrasts the variation in planets with God's consistency).

124. This type of escapism is also, no doubt, alien to these authors, who speak of "the world" as a value system elsewhere in their commentaries. See Allison, *James*, 365–66; Painter and deSilva, *James and Jude*, 199.

125. Wilkinson, *Christian Eschatology*, 5.

eschatological judgment). It is a closed system in which self-assertion is substituted for love of others, arrogance for humility, and greed for mercy.[126] In this system, the worth of human beings is measured in terms of wealth and status, thus creating either jealousy or arrogance. These attitudes then bring divisions in the social body and lead to oppression. Moreover, the κόσμος is not only an external reality, it has a seat within human beings, located in the tongue and in evil desires.

James also depicts "the world" as a spiritual entity inspired by Satan and demonic forces. As such, it is a power of death. This entity opposes God's kingdom and denies the validity of God's law. The weapons of the κόσμος are twofold: intimidation and deception. As an intimidating power, it oppresses—sometimes to the point of death—those who reject its ways. As a deceptive force, it provides people with a false sense of security through empty religion, thus preventing them from seeing reality from God's perspective and enslaving them to its worldview. With these tactics, the κόσμος hinders men and women from receiving the wisdom from above by providing them with a fallacious sense of importance. It also entices them through desires in order to create a division of the heart and lure people away from God and single-minded devotion to him.

The κόσμος in James thus always possesses a negative connotation and depicts the human race as being in opposition to God. For James, human beings are in a position of hostility towards God until they receive the wisdom from above (1:5; 3:17), the word of truth (1:18), or God's grace (4:6). In that sense, the κόσμος possesses a wide range of influence. At the same time, the realm of "the world" does *not* extend to creation: if the κόσμος affects every human being and their endeavors, it is also strictly restricted to humanity. The rest of the created order is the place where human corruption happens, but it does not belong to the κόσμος itself.

Now that we understand what James means by κόσμος, we can turn to the way *friendship* with the κόσμος, and friendship with God, function in his letter.

---

126. On the relationship between envy, arrogance, and viewing the world as a "closed system with finite resources," see Johnson, *Letter of James*, 254.

3

Friendship with God and Friendship with the Κόσμος in James

INTRODUCTION

IN THE PREVIOUS CHAPTER, I discussed the meaning of "the world" and demonstrated that James uses the word in a coherent way. In order to understand what "friendship with the world" means for James, we must now examine the ancient concept of friendship, a concept which evoked in the mind of any ancient reader a cluster of images alien to modern readers. As we will see, friendship was understood not so much in terms of intimacy, but rather in terms of reciprocal commitment and obligation.[1] I will begin by offering a summary of the essential features of the concept of friendship in the first century, and then discuss the concrete implications for our understanding of what James means by "friendship with the world" and "friendship with God."

Since Jewish texts do not provide sufficient evidence for reconstructing a comprehensive concept of friendship, the present section draws extensively on Greco-Roman literature. This is not to say that Jews did not appreciate deep quality of relationship, but their writings do not deal with the topic in depth. Jewish texts provide primarily indirect evidence, mainly

---

1. "Never in antiquity, so far as I am aware, is the revelation of personal intimacies described as necessary to the formation of friendship." Konstan, *Friendship*, 15.

derived from narratives.² Of course, the Book of Proverbs includes some aphorisms on friendship, but they are never developed. While Ben Sira contains some longer discussions on the topic (up to about ten verses), none of them comes close to the developed exposition of authors such as Aristotle, Plutarch, or Cicero. Moreover, Jewish authors in the Hellenistic and Roman periods were deeply influenced by Greek writers on the theme of friendship.³ Whenever Jewish texts add a notable contribution to a particular topic, depart from Hellenistic ideas, or stress a different point, this will be indicated.

After highlighting the essential elements of the general concept of friendship in the ancient world, we will move to the more specific idea of friendship with God. We will briefly discuss the appearance of the idea in pagan and Jewish literature before turning to the epistle of James itself to show that friendship with God has to be understood as the ideal that Christians are called to pursue. Finally, we will look at the way James employs the idea of "friendship with the world" in Jas 4:4. I will demonstrate that James denounces the willingness to embrace the ways of the κόσμος as an active rebellion against God. I will also show that James never intends his audience to withdraw from society itself.

FRIENDSHIP IN THE ANCIENT WORLD
Essential Elements⁴

It is a well-known fact that Greeks and Romans possessed the highest appreciation for friendship. Two quotations will suffice to illustrate the extent to which they valued it. According to the playwright Menander, "there is no possession lovelier than a friend."⁵ Cicero expressed a similar sentiment: "next to goodness itself, I entreat you to regard friendship as the finest thing in all the world."⁶

---

2. To my knowledge, the only book-length treatment of friendship in the Hebrew Scripture is Olyan, *Friendship*.

3. See Stählin, "Φίλος, Φίλη, Φιλία," 9:146–71.

4. The following discussion is only a brief survey, stressing the elements that are necessary to a proper understanding of James. For a very thorough exposition of friendship in the ancient world, see Konstan, *Friendship*. For other surveys, see Batten, "Unworldly Friendship," 15–127; Baltzly and Eliopoulos, "Classical Ideals of Friendship," 1–64.

5. Menander, *Sentences* 575, quoted in Konstan, *Friendship*, 57.

6. This is the concluding sentence of Cicero's discussion of friendship (*Amic.*).

Friendship was extolled by ancient authors and discussed at length by philosophers. Although each philosophical school had its specific understanding of the joys and duties of friendship, a number of core values were shared by all. Assumptions about the way friends were expected to behave pervaded the whole of society and were not restricted to the literate or the wealthy.[7]

The essential features of friendship evolved as the political setting of each period shaped society. Some of these features became more important in some periods, some less, and some remained unchanged. Four elements at least—reciprocity, a friend as another self, the connection between virtue and friendship, and the importance of choosing one's friend(s) wisely—remained foundational to people's understanding of friendship throughout antiquity.

Reciprocity

First of all, friendship presupposed reciprocity. Verboven's remark that reciprocity is "ubiquitous in Roman literature" could be extended to classical literature in general.[8] It was so central to Aristotle that he defined friendship as reciprocal goodwill (*Eth. nic.* 8.2). Since friendly relationships were marked by specific actions rather than the display of emotions, such a goodwill was demonstrated in very concrete ways. Friends had the moral obligation to strengthen the existing bond of friendship by means of concrete gifts and attentions: "Mutuality is central to the relationship."[9] Indeed, one of the most common Greek proverbs about friendship states that friends share their possessions (κοινὰ τὰ φίλων, already cited by Aristotle in *Eth. nic.* 9.8.2 as common knowledge and further quoted by Cicero, Seneca, Plutarch, and Philo).[10] This mutual sharing of goods was particularly

---

Cicero, *On the Good Life*, 227.

7. See Evans, "Friendship," 181–202. Evans concludes that no notable difference in the expectations of friendship is to be found among different social groups, except that there is no record of friendship among slaves or the poor. However, the lack of record does not entail the nonexistence of friendship among these groups.

8. Verboven, "Friendship," 405.

9. Konstan, "Reciprocity," 284.

10. According to Luke Timothy Johnson, this element of friendship especially comes to the fore in the NT in the description of the early church (Acts 2:44–45; 4:32–37) and in Paul's letter to the Philippians. Johnson, "Making Connections," 161–65.

important in classical times when society was still composed of family-size estates, since it represented the only insurance against bankruptcy.

Friends also helped or protected one another in times of need (Aristotle *Eth. nic.* 8.1; Plutarch *Amic. mult.* 3; cf. Prov 27:19; Sir 6:14; 37:5; Luke 11:5–8). Hence, David Konstan notes that "the fear of betrayal centres largely on the failure of friends to provide help in emergencies, indicating that one of the chief values of friendship was assistance."[11] In other words, loyalty to one's friends—not breaking the circle of reciprocity—was viewed as an all-important virtue (Sir 6:8–10). This was so important that giving one's life was almost thought of as a natural aspect of true friendship.[12] Jewish texts completely concurred with Hellenistic ones on all of this (see Sir 27:16; 22:23; 37:5–6; in Philo, see *Plant.* 106; *Prob.* 85–88; *Hypot.* 11:4, 10–13).

The Friend as Another Self

Friendship also implied sharing similar interests, values, and worldviews. According to Cicero, "friendship may be defined as a complete identity of feeling about all things in heaven and earth."[13] This view is also captured in another famous proverb: "friends are one soul" (μία ψυχή).[14] Here lies the heart of true friendship: "he and I shared all the same interests. Our tastes and aims and views were identical and that is where the essence of a friendship must always lie."[15] This aspect results from the fact that "friendships are formed on the basis of individual association, as opposed to ties of kinship or citizenship or some other formal status" and therefore possess a voluntary character.[16] Although it may sound self-evident, philosophical treatments of friendship—Stoic ones in particular—insisted on this aspect. For them, the "core of the friendship is not warm feelings of affection, but like-mindedness or *homonoia*—commitment to the cause."[17] Obviously,

---

11. Konstan, "Reciprocity," 287.

12. See, for instance, Cicero, *Amic.* 7.24; Jesus in John 15:13. See also Konstan, *Friendship*, 59.

13. Cicero, *On the Good Life*, 187.

14. *Eth. nic.* 9.8.2; *Eth. eud.* 7.6.10. The same expression is found in Euripides, *Orest.* 1046. A similar idea appears in in *Eth. nic.* 9.4; Plutarch, *Amic. mult.* 8.

15. *Amic.* 4.14, quoted in Mews, "Cicero on Friendship," 70. Cf. Plutarch, *Adul. amic.* 6; *Amic. mult.* 8.

16. Konstan, "Patrons and Friends," 332.

17. Baltzly and Eliopoulos, "Classical Ideals of Friendship," 35.

this can happen only insofar as friends share the same ideal and help one another to embody it: "the society [i.e. company] of the good may supply a sort of training in goodness."[18] Classical authors stressed not only the idea that virtuous friends improve one another, but also the negative corollary: bad company results in moral corruption. Here also, Jews agreed entirely (Sir 6:17; in Philo, see *Her.* 83; *Det.* 33; *Virt.* 103). A shared commitment to moral values or to an ideal is essential, because ancients agreed that one of the greatest benefits of friendship was the ability to have one's character perfected by one's friends.

Friendship and Virtue

The idea that friendship is only possible among virtuous people can be derived as a logical conclusion of the idea explored in the previous paragraph. Aristotle describes three types of friendship, which depend on what the two individuals seek in the relationship: utility, pleasure, or virtue (*Eth. nic.* 8.2–3). Although anyone can be a "friend" for the sake of utility (two people doing business together) or pleasure (enjoying the same kind of activity), Aristotle maintains that friendship cannot be complete—nor last over time—unless the two persons are endowed with a virtuous character. All three types are described as friendship (φίλια), but only the last type is considered perfect (τέλειος) and able to last: "perfect friendship is the friendship of men who are good, and alike in virtue" (*Eth. nic.* 8.3; see also *Eth. Eud.* 7.2.15-17). "This kind of friendship, then, is perfect both in respect of duration and in all other respects" (*Eth. nic.* 8.4). Cicero's view, expressed three centuries later, is remarkably similar: "friendship is only possible between good men."[19] He is even more explicit later: "What unites friends in the first place . . . and what keeps them friends, is goodness of character. All harmony, and permanence, and fidelity, come from that."[20]

Choosing Friends Wisely and "Testing" Friendship

Another steady feature of friendship is that one should be careful in choosing friends. Because friendship was so highly regarded, it was especially important not to offer one's friendship lightly.[21] Only fools would enter

---

18. Aristotle, quoting Theognis in *Eth. nic.* 9.9.7.
19. Cicero, *On the Good Life*, 185. See also Plutarch, *Amic. mult.* 3.
20. Cicero, *On the Good Life*, 224–25.
21. Plutarch, *Amic. mult.* 3–5. See also the discussion on Plutarch in Baltzly and

into a new friendship before being well acquainted with the other's character. Cicero laments that "an immense amount of care is devoted to acquiring the cattle, but none... to choosing friends."[22] He continues by saying that one should "subject his friends to the same sort of preliminary testing operation that men apply to their horses."[23]

This is not to say that people would actively trick others. These authors simply invite their readers to let circumstances—especially times of need—reveal the hidden aspects of a person's character. "Circumstances [*kairos*] test friends, just as fire tests gold."[24] Therefore, true friendship can only develop through time, as the character of each person is gradually revealed or confirmed. "For a friend is not to be had without trial [πειρασμός] and is not a matter of a single day, but time is needed" (Aristotle, *Eth. Eud.* 7.2.46). Jewish authors did not differ in that respect. For instance, Ben Sira uses very similar language when he exclaims, "if you acquire a friend, acquire him through testing" (Sir 6:7).

This last quotation comes from a section (Sir 6:5–17) in which Ben Sira contrasts the loyal friend (φίλος πιστός) who remains faithful in adversity (Sir 6:14–16) with the flatterer who fakes friendship for the sake of material gain (Sir 6:5, 8–12). The concern to distinguish between the genuine friend and the greedy parasite became more and more important as the concept of friendship evolved with time. It is to that evolution that we now turn.

Evolution in Friendship: Terminology, Unequal Friends, and Frank Speech

The Greco-Roman understanding of friendship evolved over time in at least one important area: that of equality. As democratic city-states were the dominant mode of political organization in the classical era, the ideal of equality deeply influenced the definition of friendship. In this context, "equality of social station [was] a prerequisite for friendship, at all events for the ideal type of friendship."[25] Aristotle considers friendship impossible

---

Eliopoulos, "Classical Ideals of Friendship," 43.

22. Cicero, *On the Good Life*, 208.

23. Cicero, *On the Good Life*, 208–09.

24. Menander, Aphorism IX.8–9, quoted in Konstan, "Reciprocity," 286–87; see also XI.2. The same point is made in Aesop's fable "The Bear and the Two Travellers." Similar quotes can be found in Konstan, *Friendship*, 57.

25. Konstan, "Reciprocity," 290.

if the difference in status between two friends becomes too significant. Another popular saying is quoted several times and grounds his whole discussion of friendship: "friendship is equality" (φιλότης ἰσότης, *Eth. nic.* 8.5; 8.8; *Eth. eud.* 7.4; 7.8; 7.10).

However, this view of friendship was tied to the political context in which it evolved. As democracy gave place to a more pyramidal structure, unequal roles in friendship became more common.[26] At first, "having friends in high places, such as the Macedonian court, laid one open to suspicion of greed and servility."[27] Comedies often derided those who present themselves as "friends" of anyone in power; such people "were consistently referred to as 'flatterers', 'parasites', and occasionally as slaves."[28] After a transitional period, however, the new state of affairs came to be accepted, and uneven friendship became widespread during the Hellenistic period.[29] Along with this evolution, the signifier of loyalty shifted from mutual assistance in times of crisis to frank speech (παρρησία). Since those who attempted to climb into positions of influence for personal gain would rarely, if ever, take the risk of provoking a powerful friend to anger, courage to voice disagreement came to be seen as a sign of genuine interest in the good of the other. Frank speech, therefore, served to distinguish between an advisor who desired to help an official to rule well and one who was latching on to the powerful for what they could get from him.[30]

This shift occasioned an evolution of the language of friendship in two areas. First, the appearance of unequal friendship led to a blurring of the lines between genuine friendship (in which the two parties have equal appreciation for one another and are seeking the good of the other) and patronage (where the behavior of the patron can be condescending and where the client was merely seeking his own advantage). Some scholars

26. This is not to say that democracy meant complete equality—far from it. Greek democracy implied that all free male citizens could partake in the political life of the city, but some form of hierarchy also existed during that period: slaves were not considered equal to free citizens, and women were not considered equal to men. However, when Aristotle speaks of friendship, he always posits a relationship between two free citizens of similar status. Friendship between a citizen and a slave was not conceivable for Aristotle.

27. Konstan, *Friendship*, 101.

28. Herman, "Friends," 118.

29. This evolution is described in more detail in Konstan, "Reciprocity," and Konstan, "Friendship, Frankness and Flattery," 7–19.

30. Plutarch's *How to Tell a Flatterer from a Friend* (*Adul. amic.*) is written to deal with precisely that issue, and witnesses to the importance of the matter. For mention of frank speech in Philo, see *Her.* 21; *Migr.* 116.

even defend the idea that friendship was assimilated into the patron-client relationship during the Roman period. However, David Konstan demonstrates quite convincingly that the difference between friends and clients was understood and assumed throughout the Roman period.[31] It remains true, however, that friendship sometimes functioned as a euphemism for patron-client relationships, so that patrons—or benefactors—were sometimes referred to simply as "friends."

Second, the term "friend" (φίλος) was sometimes used as a political *terminus technicus*. During the Hellenistic period, φίλος often refers to an advisor of a king.[32] This title had become a common designation for court officials.[33] The language of friendship was also used in alliances. For example, the hendiadys "ally and friend" (σύμμαχος καὶ φίλος) regularly refers to political treaties.[34] Such alliances involved promises "to respect territorial integrity and . . . to provide military assistance in times of need."[35] The use of φίλος in such contexts implies loyalty—the notion of reciprocity transferred to a codified relationship between a ruler and his vassals, or even to an impersonal relationship, in the case of alliances between cities or states—but it does not presuppose anything else. The other three typical elements of friendship—virtue, sharing the same values, and testing the other's character—do not apply in such a case. Here again, the language of friendship covers an area distinct from friendship. Obviously, people in the ancient world could distinguish between interpersonal friendship and the political realities described in the same terms. Context, then, provides the key to which meaning of friendship is best reflected in a particular text.

---

31. See Konstan, "Patrons and Friends."

32. When the title is fully spelled, it reads "friend of the king," (φίλος τοῦ βασιλέως), but it is sometimes abbreviated as simply "friend." For this usage in the LXX, see 1 Macc 2:18; 3:38; 6:10, 14, 28; 7:6, 8, 15; 10:19–20, 60, 65; 11:57; 12:43; 13:36; 15:28, 32. See also 2 Macc 1:14; 7:24; 8:9; 10:13; 14:11; Esth 1:3, 13; 2:18; 3:1; 6:9; Dan 3:91, 94; 5:23; probably Dan 6:13.

33. For a full discussion, see Herman, "Friends." See also Walbank, "Monarchies," 62–100.

34. 1 Macc 8:20, 31; 10:16; 15:17. Φίλος alone is used in the same context in 1 Macc 11:33.

35. Baltzly and Eliopoulos, "Classical Ideals of Friendship," 27. See references cited there.

Preliminary Conclusion

The discussion above makes it clear that friendship was by no means a casual relationship in the first century—indeed, friendship entailed deep commitment. Moreover, character formation was tied to friendship in important ways. We saw that at least four characteristics—reciprocity, sharing a common worldview, being virtuous people, and taking time to test the character of the other—were integral to the ancient understanding of friendship and did not undergo any significant change over time. In contrast, the picture of friendship drastically evolved on the issue of equality, so that by the first century friendship between people of different social status was at least considered possible, and the language of friendship was often used as a euphemism for patronage.

FRIENDSHIP IN THE LETTER OF JAMES

We are now in a position to explore how the metaphor of friendship works in the literary context of James's letter. For this purpose, we will now look at the two key expressions essential to a proper understanding of James 4:4, namely "friendship with the world" and "friendship with God."

Friendship with "the World" in James

Now that the concepts of κόσμος and friendship have been studied, we move to define "friendship with the world." Quite clearly, not all four elements composing the ideal friendship will play a role in this definition. Typically, the idea of choosing one's friends wisely cannot be in view at all, nor the idea that friendship and virtue are connected.[36] This suggests that the political use of φιλία—friendship as a euphemism for patronage or rewarded allegiance—may be what James has in view with the concept of "friendship with the world."

The elements of reciprocity and identity of interest, on the other hand, certainly do play an important role in the meaning of "friendship with the world." The notion that friendship implies reciprocity highlights the fact that the world has a way to reward its friends, probably by providing status and privilege. This would find parallels in other wisdom texts that describe

---

36. James 3:15 implies that an "earthly wisdom" exists, though—interestingly—he never speaks of it explicitly. The noun has to be supplied from the expression "wisdom from above." The context makes clear that "earthly wisdom" is no "wisdom" at all but rather an "anti-wisdom."

the wicked as immune to difficult circumstances (e.g., Pss 49, 73). Like those who court the powerful, the "friend of the world" hopes to get some benefits from the relationship.[37] If "friendship with the world" uses the political overtone of friendship, then the idea of identity of interests receives the connotation of complete compliance to the values and interests of the more powerful party—the κόσμος. To be a "friend of the world" implies adopting all the views and goals of the κόσμος. In particular, it entails a life shaped by the two hallmarks of the κόσμος—failure to control one's tongue (Jas 1:26; 3:6) and envy (Jas 4:1–4). As Johnson puts it, to be "'friends of the world,' then, means to live by the logic of envy, rivalry, competition, and murder."[38] Positioning oneself as "friend of the world" implies a strong commitment to the world's values—and therefore an implicit opposition to God and his kingdom. It means seeking one's status rather than showing mercy, being content with empty words of comfort rather than providing the poor with what they need, and arrogantly affirming oneself rather than seeking peace.

Since the κόσμος was defined in the last chapter as the realm in which the reality of God, his promises, and his commands is not considered, to be a "friend of the world" is to "lead one's life as though God had no claim on it."[39] It is an attempt to secure one's life apart from God by refusing to trust God's grace (Jas 4:6) and receive from him the gifts he provides (Jas 1:17). Friendship with the world either fails to recognize the human need for God and his gift of wisdom, or actively refuses to acknowledge it.

The significant shift of tone from exhortation to severe condemnation in Jas 4:1 alerts us to another element of friendship with the κόσμος.[40] Lacking the courage to distance oneself from the dominant value system is reproved in Jas 2, and such a failure represents a hindrance to pursuing friendship with God. Nevertheless, it does not yet imply a full association with the "world," because the behavior likely stems from weakness. In contrast, chapter 4 presents conscious connivance with the κόσμος on the basis of envy. It attacks the *willingness* of those who "want to be friends of the world" (βουληθῇ φίλος εἶναι τοῦ κόσμου, 4:4). In James, the verb βούλομαι

---

37. This is more or less the view proposed in Batten, *Friendship*. For Batten, however, the idea that the community can benefit from "the world" means they are tempted to rely on wealthy patrons. It seems to me that this narrows the possibility of a reward from "the world" far too much.

38. Johnson, *Letter of James: A New Translation*, 251.

39. Johnson, "Friendship," 216.

40. See section titled "Κόσμος in James 4:4" on pp. 32–38.

always has the meaning of a resolve, a decision.[41] Here it also conveys also the idea of a deliberate association with the κόσμος; these people "establish themselves" in that position (καθίσταται, read as a middle, as in 3:6).[42] The language of friendship—implying, as we have seen, complete commitment—and of double-mindedness (δίψυχος, 4:8) needs to be taken seriously. It implies that "friendship with the world" describes the fundamental attitude and orientation of the person. James presents the transformation of one's fundamental allegiance not as a gradual process but as a choice, an act of the will. The repentance James calls for amounts to taking a clear stance against "the world."

Moreover, since James defines the κόσμος as the value system opposed to God's royal law (2:8), and summarizes the law in the double commandment to love God (1:12; 2:5) and to love one's neighbor (2:8), it appears that rejecting the κόσμος designates a firm stance against anything that stands in the way of loving one's neighbor. Positioning oneself against "the world" is James's way of speaking about the quality that other wisdom texts label "hatred of evil."[43] Consequently, refusing to become a "friend of the world"— or, in the language of 1:27, remaining "unstained from the world"—can be defined as an absolute commitment not to let anything hinder love for one's neighbor. Nothing, no matter how culturally acceptable, has the right to take precedence over the royal law of love and mercy.

Friendship as a Relationship between Individuals

We should here make explicit an aspect of friendship that has thus far remained implicit—namely that friendship was in ancient times, as it is today, a bond between individuals.[44] This fact is so obvious that it often

---

41. Cf. Jas 1:18 (God's will) and 3:4 (will of the pilot).

42. Johnson also stresses the aspect of decision. He especially underlines the force of the verb καθίστημι which, he says, "has almost an official tone." Johnson, "Friendship," 211. See also Adamson, *Epistle of James*, 170.

43. Hatred of evil is regularly seen in Scripture as an integral part of the fear of God. See especially Prov 8:13; cf. Pss 34:13-14; 36:4; 45:8; 97:10; 101:3; Amos 5:15; Rom 12:9; 1 Thess 5:21-22; 1 Pet 3:10-11; Rev 2:2.

44. It is true that friendship sometimes formed the basis for communal living. This was the case especially among Epicurean schools and their famous "community of friends," which has sometimes been compared to the early Christian communities. (See, for instance, Baltzly and Eliopoulos, "Classical Ideals of Friendship," 41.) Even in that case, however, "friendship remains a bond between individuals," even if "it is communally fostered and exploited in the service of philosophical instruction and development."

goes unnoticed, but it reveals an important aspect of James's theology. Throughout his epistle, James shows special concern for community life. The metaphor of friendship, however, singles out individual members of the community: choosing friendship with the κόσμος or friendship with God is a decision of an individual. To be sure, this choice has communal consequences, but it remains an individual choice all the same. Every single member of the community has a duty to position him- or herself against "the world."

Since friendship is an image that involves individuals, evil must be fought at the individual level, inside each person. In other words, James does not depict evil as a systemic issue, but as a personal one. Given that the κόσμος has a seat within the person (3:6), transforming society is impossible unless the human hearts of individual people are transformed. This is confirmed by Jas 4:1, which claims that struggles come from inner desires.[45] While evil has clear communal and systemic consequences, these cannot be solved at a societal level; they are the symptoms, not the root, of the real problem. This has important consequences for the way James understands the relationship between the church and society which will be explored in the next chapter. For now, we can simply say that this last point accounts for James's consistent focus on the community. Such a narrow focus does not does not stem from a disregard for those who do not belong to the community, but from a belief that real transformation is possible *only* in the community of those who welcome the word of truth (1:21) and the wisdom from above (3:17).

Excursus 1: Friendship with God and Separation from "the World"

Because this last point is not always seen clearly, some scholars have reasoned from the narrow focus on the community to the view that separation from "the world" implies a sectarian stance. Though this idea has not won many adherents, it still appears regularly in scholarly publications and would impact the reading of James's epistle in a major way if upheld. We therefore offer a fuller response to that position.

The exegesis performed in Chapter 2 showed that the rejection of the κόσμος need not be interpreted in a sectarian way at all. First, James always

---

Konstan, *Friendship*, 113.

45. Again, see discussion in the preceding chapter.

speaks of "the world" as a value system, a worldview, or a way of being, never as a location in space. Second, since the κόσμος has a foothold within the individual (see our discussion of Jas 3:6), it is impossible to escape it by separating oneself from those who do not belong to the community. A group withdrawing from society would simply bring "the world" with it.

The aim of this section is to provide additional grounds on which to reject the sectarian reading of James. We will examine the arguments of those who think that rejection of the κόσμος implies a withdrawal from society, respond to these arguments, and offer textual evidence that James does not presuppose a sectarian community.

Scholars Defending a Sectarian Stance in James's Letter

Leo Perdue presents an argument based on his interpretation of the social setting and function of paraenetic literature. In his first article related to the epistle of James, he contends that "the paraenesis of James exhorts the audience to reflect upon their initial entrance into the community, *to continue to dissociate themselves from the world*, and to engage in more committed efforts to strive towards a higher level of virtue and perfection."[46] In a second article, he goes even further and describes James as an example of what he calls "subversive paraenesis," which aims at undermining "the legitimacy of the prevailing order of the society."[47] He believes that the recipients of James's letter withdrew from the wider society to gather into a small community ("Gemeinschaft"), in which "a different social reality is constructed and efforts are undertaken to protect it from the threat of outside worlds."[48] For him, the epistle of James is "a good example of this *sectarian position*."[49] Perdue, however, does not ground his observation in the text. He merely compares the purposes of different paraenetic writings in order to classify them, and asserts his opinion concerning the letter of James without defending it.[50]

---

46. Perdue, "Paraenesis," 250–51 (emphasis mine).
47. Perdue, "Social Character," 26.
48. Perdue, "Social Character," 26.
49. Perdue, "Social Character," 26 (emphasis mine).
50. Other scholars follow the same line of thought of Perdue. See for instance Witherington, *Jesus the Sage*, 246. Despite disagreeing with Perdue on the kind of wisdom James advocates ("his is basically *not* a Wisdom of counter order," 238), Witherington nevertheless concludes that James's imperatives are meant "to inculcate a community with carefully controlled boundaries." He grounds his conclusion in Malina's cultural

John Elliott develops the same idea from another angle, namely a socio-rhetorical analysis of the epistle. According to Elliott, James's epistle centers around purity language with the goal to set clear boundaries around the community and "to undergird an ethic of holy non-conformity."[51] James contrasts the "wisdom from above" and an "earthly wisdom" that define "two distinct and opposing realms of the cosmos."[52] This division in turn "demarcates and contrasts *two societies* inspired by two opposed sources and forms of wisdom."[53] Since Elliott equates wholeness and purity, he believes that the only way to wholeness is to stay away from impurity—that is, from the society shaped by the wisdom of below. Staying pure thus implies staying away from contact with that society. To be fair to Elliott, he never claims in unambiguous terms that the community must withdraw from contact with the rest of society to achieve purity, but this is what his article seems to imply. In any case, his article is usually interpreted in that way.[54] Elliott won a notable follower in the person of Robert Wall, who asserts that the command "to remain unstained from the world" (ἄσπιλον ἑαυτὸν τηρεῖν ἀπὸ τοῦ κόσμου) in Jas 1:27 should be interpreted as a sectarian separation from society.[55]

Analysis and Response

Elliott's description of the wisdom of below as a polluting influence can certainly be accepted. However, his argument rests on the *assumption* that remaining pure implies complete separation from society and not only from its values. The same can be said of Perdue's understanding of paraenesis and of Wall's comment that James champions a "sectarian asceticism" in Jas 1:26–27.[56] This conjecture, however, does not bear closer scrutiny. As we saw, the κόσμος is defined in James in terms of values and practices, not in terms of physical or social place. Therefore, whereas remaining "unstained from the world" (1:27) does represent a major emphasis in James's letter, withdrawing from society does not. These scholars offer a simplistic and

---

anthropology.
51. Elliott, "Holiness-Wholeness," 79.
52. Elliott, "Holiness-Wholeness," 77.
53. Elliott, "Holiness-Wholeness," 77 (emphasis mine).
54. See especially Lockett's critique of Elliott. Lockett, *Purity and Worldview*, 13–17.
55. Wall, *Community*, 98.
56. Wall, *Community*, 101.

unhelpful model of interaction between the community and the society in which it was found.

A more nuanced and promising way forward has been sketched by Darian Lockett in his analysis of James's cultural stance.[57] Lockett grounds his analysis in John Barclay's model of social interaction in Diaspora Judaism, which distinguishes between "assimilation" (measuring social interaction), "acculturation" (measuring the level of acquaintance with Greco-Roman culture, education, literature, and values), and "accommodation" (measuring the acceptance or rejection of what is known of the Greco-Roman culture).[58] Looking at these three characteristics in James's letter, Lockett concludes that the author "is plainly acculturated with respect to language, rhetoric, values, and some intellectual traditions" and does not, therefore, reject every cultural aspect of his context.[59] Rather, he adopts a significant numbers of features typical of Hellenistic Judaism and Greco-Roman culture in general. Lockett also observes that James never depicts the audience as an "in-group" contrasted with those who would be outside of the community; typical boundary markers—circumcision and the like—are remarkably absent in the letter.[60] Hence, James never discourages or limits social interactions. When it comes to accommodation, Locket considers most the content of the letter to be "culturally neutral," but points out that James resists the general attitude of his culture on the topics of one's relationship with the poor and the proper use of the tongue, the two elements that James explicitly associates with the pollution of "the world."[61] Using Barclay's model of social interaction allows for a more nuanced approach to the wider culture.

Textual Arguments against a Sectarian Community

The epistle provides further evidence that James does not intend community members to withdraw from interaction with people who are not part of the community. Two main arguments point in that direction.

---

57. See Chapter 5, "Purity and the Cultural Stance of James," in Lockett, *Purity and Worldview*, 147–84; Lockett, "Strong and Weak Lines," 391–405.

58. See Barclay, "Diaspora Environment," 82–102.

59. Lockett, *Purity and Worldview*, 181.

60. Lockett, "Strong and Weak Lines," 398–400.

61. Lockett, "Strong and Weak Lines," 401. On the same two elements, see also Davids, "Controlling the Tongue," 225–47.

First, most of the commands implying human relationships are not restricted to the community. To be sure, some passages explicitly refer to other community members (Jas 2:15; 4:11; 5:13, 19), but the majority have a universal import. This comes out most clearly in 3:9, where the idea that human beings are made in God's image is invoked as reason for not cursing others. The same may also be true of 1:27, where James speaks of "God and Father" (ὁ θεὸς καὶ πατήρ) in order to stress the universal brotherhood of humanity.[62] In 2:2–4, the logic of the argument implies that the two men entering the community do not belong to it (if they did, they would know where to sit).[63] This further implies that the objects of the commands to love one's neighbor (2:8) and to show mercy (2:13) should not be restricted to members of the community. Finally, the definition of the wisdom from above (3:13–18) applies to any human relationship. Admittedly, Jas 3 mainly speaks of divisions among the letter's recipients, and the qualities describing the wisdom from above in 3:17–18 (gentleness, willingness to submit, compassion, impartiality, sincerity, peace-making) are primarily the means of reconciliation and the building up of a strong, peaceful community. However, Jas 3:9–12 points to pure speech towards any human being and invites the reader to speak words of life, symbolized by fresh water and good fruits (3:11–12). Moreover, wisdom literature in general aims at shaping the whole of life, and James's letter is no exception. "A believer consistently characterized by these virtues would truly impact the world for God's kingdom."[64]

Second, many passages of the letter indicate that James conceives of his readers as being involved in society. For instance, in 4:13–17 James rebukes merchants for their confidence that everything depends on them, yet, he does not condemn business in itself. As Thomas More Garrett writes, "the passage is not a straightforward condemnation of business activity. Commentators agree that James is denouncing neither commercial activity itself nor profit-seeking more generally."[65] James condemns not commerce but the arrogance of the merchants' attitude and—as we will demonstrate in the next chapter—the failure of these merchants to help the poor in

---

62. See especially Ng, "Father-God Language," 41–54. See also Davids, *Epistle of James*, 103; Adamson, *Epistle of James*, 86.

63. See Laws, *James*, 99–100.

64. Blomberg and Kamell, *James*, 176.

65. Garrett, "Message to the Merchants," 301. See note 5 for a list of commentators agreeing on this.

proportion to their wealth.⁶⁶ For our present purpose, it is sufficient to note that James assumes that some members of the community will travel in order to engage in trade. Furthermore, the following section of James implies that other members of the community are working as labourers in the fields of rich landowners. The "righteous one" (ὁ δίκαιος) in 5:6 is most likely a "generic collective term" standing for whoever practices God's will.⁶⁷ In short, the letter provides evidence that many members were active in professions that imply close contact with outsiders. Johnson summarizes the matter well: James "envisages Christians taking full part in the affairs of the world: commerce, landowning, judging, owning and distributing possessions, having houses for hospitality."⁶⁸

These considerations demonstrate that James does not wish for opposition to the κόσμος to take the shape of a sectarian withdrawal from human society. He assumes that believers will continue to live within a corrupt society, yet in a distinctive way, especially when it comes to matters of money and of speech ethics.

FRIENDSHIP WITH GOD

The other expression we need to define is "friendship with God." Although the expression never appears as such in James's epistle, it is clear that Jas 4:4 presupposes it. The language of "friendship with the world" and "enmity with God" present in that verse implies that the readers are implicitly invited to develop a "friendship with God" rather than with "the world."

Before looking at its use in James's epistle, we will first discuss what the expression means when it is found in other contemporary texts, with the goal of gaining a better grasp on what "friendship with God" meant in the first century.

---

66. On the condemnation of arrogance, see especially McKnight, *James*, 368–79.

67. Davids, *Epistle of James*, 179. Other scholars see this as a reference to James the Just, taking the letter to be written shortly after his death. See for instance Martin, *James*, 186. Still others see a reference to Jesus. See Witherington, *Letters*, 530. Reading "the righteous" as a singular collective makes good sense and is the most straightforward reading.

68. Johnson, "Friendship," 212.

Friendship with God in the Greco-Roman World

Just as people's understanding of friendship evolved, the idea of friendship with God developed over time. Erik Peterson laid the framework for all subsequent work on this subject almost a century ago. Peterson argued that two streams of ideas coexisted among the Greeks: one in which friendship between human beings and gods was considered possible, and one in which it was not.[69] The paradigm was generally accepted among biblical scholars until 1996. After several decades without any debate, David Konstan challenged Peterson's conclusion. Looking at a variety of texts, Konstan shows that Greeks made a strong distinction between "a friend" (the *substantive* φίλος, often articular) and someone being dear to someone else (the relationship is described by φιλία and sometimes the *adjective* φίλος).[70] To illustrate his point, Konstan gives the following example: "one may observe that a mother may love her son and be loved by him, but it would be absurd on this basis alone to call them lovers."[71] With this distinction, Konstan shows that the vast majority of texts allegedly speaking of friendship between a god and a human being merely referred to a hero being "dear" to a god, usually for some virtue championed by the god in question. Only around the turn of the era—and only among Stoic philosophers—do we find some hints of the possibility of friendship between the wise and the gods.[72] In that context, the stress falls on the idea that the sage shares some divine characteristics, especially freedom (ἐλευθερία).[73] This type of expression, however, remains extremely rare in pagan literature.

Friendship with God in Second Temple Judaism

The idea that friendship with God is possible is found almost exclusively in Judaism and Christianity, and is grounded in a few biblical passages.[74] Once the possibility is established, however, the consequences of such a

---

69. Peterson, "Der Gottesfreund," 161–202. Aristotle is the archetypal champion of the latter view, on the grounds that the difference of power between the two parties—breaking the rule of equality—makes friendship between gods and humans impossible.

70. Konstan, "Problems," 91–94. The same argument appears in Konstan, "Greek Friendship," 71–94; Konstan, *Friendship*, 167–70.

71. Konstan, "Greek Friendship," 76.

72. Konstan, "Problems," 94–95.

73. Epictetus, *Diatr.* 2.17.27, 4.3.9, cited in Konstan, "Problems," 95.

74. See Konstan, "Problems," 95–96; Batten, *Friendship*, 48–55.

relationship draw heavily from the Hellenistic ideal of friendship, as we will see.

In the biblical text, the relationship of Moses with God is *compared* with friendship in Exod 33:11, and Abraham is described as being "the one being dear to you [God]" in 2 Chr 20:7.[75] Inspired by these passages, Abraham[76] and Moses[77] are then regularly presented as friends of God. Following Wis 7:27, "the wise" are also afforded this honorific title from time to time.[78] One should note that in this verse friendship with God is both a gift (it comes as the result of the reception of the gift of wisdom) and a process. The verb "to prepare" (κατασκευάζω) conveys the idea of a set of concrete actions that happen over time rather than the bestowal of an appellation given once and for all.[79] The common feature of all these references is that the title "friends of God" is reserved for paradigmatic models of piety and is always related to the godliness of the character bearing the title.

Philo—the only writer who repeatedly uses the language of friendship with God—employs the epithet "friend of God" to stress one of three elements. Most frequently, friendship with God underlines the idea that someone shares God's character or thought. Thus, friends of God are able to see things only God can see (*Leg.* 3:71) and to distinguish good from evil because God shares his knowledge with them (*Somn.* 2:296). They alone are faithful, just as God is faithful (*Leg.* 3:204). Friends of God, being perfectly

---

75. In Exod 33:11, God speaks to Moses "as a man speaks to his friend" (MT: כַּאֲשֶׁ֛ר יְדַבֵּ֥ר אִ֖ישׁ אֶל־רֵעֵ֑הוּ; LXX: ὡς εἴ τις λαλήσει πρὸς τὸν ἑαυτοῦ φίλον). 2 Chr 20:7 speaks of Abraham being "dear to you [God]" (MT: אַבְרָהָ֥ם אֹֽהַבְךָ֖; LXX: Αβρααμ τῷ ἠγαπημένῳ σου). See also Gen 18:7. LXX adds "my servant" (ὁ παῖς μου) to the MT; Philo *Sobr.* 56 adds "my friend" (ὁ φίλος μου) to his citation of Gen. 18:7; *Tg. Neof.* does the same as Philo.

76. See Philo *Sobr.* 56; *Abr.* 87, 235, 273; *Virt.* 218; *Jub.* 19:9; *T. Ab.* [A] 1:6; 2:3; 4:7; 8:2, 4; 9:7; 15:12, 13, 14; 16:5, 9; 20:14; *T. Ab.* 4:10; 8:2; 13:1, 5; *1 Clem* 10:1; 17:2; Irenaeus, *Haer.* 4.14.4; 16.2; Tertullian, *Adv. Jud.* 2:7.

77. See Philo *Ebr.* 94; *Sacr.* 130; *Migr.* 45; *Mos.* 1:156.

78. "[Wisdom] enters pious souls and prepares them [to be] friends of God and prophets" ([σοφία] εἰς ψυχὰς ὁσίας μεταβαίνουσα φίλους θεοῦ καὶ προφήτας κατασκευάζει·). See also Philo *Leg.* 3:1, 74, 204; *Her.* 21; *Somn.* 2:219, 2:297; *Prob.* 42, 44. Cf. *Jub.* 30:21. Other figures are rarely afforded the title, but a few other biblical heroes receive it. According to Batten (*Friendship*, 54), Isaac and Jacob are mentioned as "friends of God" in the Damascus Document (CD 3:2).

79. Κατασκευάζω is the most common compound of σκευάζω and, at least originally, "must have been felt as intensive, 'to equip [fully], prepare [thoroughly].'" The intensive force of compounds is, however, sometimes lost and always difficult to assess. See Silva, "Κατασκευάζω," 2:642.

virtuous, are free (*Prob.* 42; *Sobr.* 55–56) and God shares his authority with them (*Prob.* 42)—in particular, they are free from vain glory (*Sobr.* 57), desires, and anger (*Prob.* 45). Second, Philo twice claims that God's friends possess all things. Because they despise the goods of this world and because "friends have all in common" (κοινὰ τὰ φίλων), friends of God receive the whole world in inheritance (*Sobr.* 55–56; *Mos.* 1:155–57).[80] Though the emphasis falls on the idea that true riches are not material goods but virtue, it is still notable that Philo would speak of material consequences of one's friendship with God. Third, friends of God enjoy, like Moses, great boldness (παρρησία) in their prayers (*Her.* 19–21). These three points give us a fuller picture of what friendship with God would evoke for first-century Jews, and demonstrate that it presupposes a great commitment to him.

Ben Sira also understands friendship with God as exceptional. He, too, regards it as the end result of a long process, and he particularly stresses the importance of times of testing. According to William Irwin, Ben Sira presents God as a faithful friend who tests people's character before committing himself to friendship—as was expected of any wise person in the ancient world.[81] The possibility of enjoying God's friendship thus hinges, in Ben Sira, on one's response to difficult circumstances:

> When the suffering of one who fears God is put in the context of friendship, the traditional concept of divine testing takes on a different look. It becomes a stage in the ordinary progress of friendship through faithfulness to complete trust.... If God tests, it is not, as may be supposed, by inflicting suffering, but, like ordinary human beings, by being wise enough to realize that few actually remain friends in adverse circumstances and prove themselves worthy of full confidence.[82]

The process through which friendship with God develops is the new element Ben Sira brings to the description offered so far.[83]

To summarize, it is clear that friendship with God was considered possible in first-century Judaism, and that the concept was derived from

---

80. Apparently, Philo is here indebted to a syllogism of the Cynic philosopher Diogenes quoted by Diogenes Laertius, *Lives* 6.72. The same argument is repeated by Clement of Alexandria, *Protr.* 12.122.10. See Konstan, *Friendship*, 169.

81. See Irwin, "Fear of God," 551–59. Irwin is followed by Corley, "Friendship According to Ben Sira," 65–72.

82. Irwin, "Fear of God," 558.

83. As we saw, the same idea is also present, albeit indirectly, in Wis 7:27.

a few texts of the Tanakh. Friendship with God is *always* understood as an ideal, a quality of relationship toward which the faithful strive, but that can be claimed by few. It is developed over time by those who—like Abraham, Job, or Elijah—remain faithful under trials and let difficult times strengthen their character and trust in God. Moreover, because God's friends share his thoughts and affections, friendship tacitly implies the effectiveness of their prayers.

Before turning to an assessment of friendship with God in James, one brief assessment of Alicia Batten's work on the concept of friendship in James is necessary. Batten published an entire monograph on the topic of friendship in James, and her work is the most extensive on the subject.[84]

Excursus 2: God as Divine Benefactor

Friendship was sometimes used in the first century as a euphemism for patronage, and Batten defends the idea that James encourages his readers to think of God as their only patron, or benefactor. According to her, James depicts God "as an ideal benefactor, on whom the audience must rely."[85] She argues that, since "it was common in the Greco-Roman world for patrons and clients to refer to one another as φίλος or *amicus*," it makes good sense to assume the same connection in James.[86] Hence, she reads Jas 3:13–4:10 as an invitation to rely on God—the only faithful provider—rather than on humans benefactors. Batten proposes three additional arguments for her thesis. First, she proposes reading Jas 2:1–13 as a denunciation of the system of human patronage. Second, noting that benefactors were sometimes referred to as "fathers," she believes that applying the term "father" to God in 1:27 and 3:9 led the audience to think of God as a benefactor. Finally, she notes that, given the connection between God and benefactors elsewhere in James, the word χάρις (used twice in 4:6) takes the connotation of "practical favour."[87]

Batten's proposal, however, faces two important difficulties that render her proposal quite unlikely. First, she is not able to provide other ancient

---

84. Batten, *Friendship*.
85. Batten, "Patron or Benefactor?," 257.
86. Batten, "Patron or Benefactor?," 259.
87. Batten, "Patron or Benefactor?," 271. Batten argues her case more carefully than can be elaborated here, but there is no need to deal with it point by point. The succinct summary provided here represents her view faithfully, I think, albeit in a simplified version.

examples where friendship *with* God functions as a means to secure material needs. As we have seen from Philo, Ben Sira, and Wisdom, Jewish writers used the title "friend of God" in quite a coherent way, but none of these references point to the usage of patronage. Batten tries to bypass this difficulty by proposing that other "biblical texts . . . explicitly use the language of benefaction to describe God," but even this is problematic.[88] None of them uses the language of benefaction with that of friendship. Moreover, neither the LXX nor the NT use the word "benefactor" (εὐεργέτης) to speak of God. Apart from Philo,[89] Jewish and Christian authors are reluctant to use the title εὐεργέτης for God.[90] Batten also appeals to the septuagintal usage of words from the extended family of the εὐεργ- root, but this does not support her assertion either. Words deriving from the εὐεργ- root are not frequent in the LXX: one finds twenty-four occurrences, with only nine of these referring to God.[91] Of these nine verses, only one (Wis 16:2) speaks of material benefits; all the others refer rather to salvation or deliverance.[92]

Second, Batten's proposal misreads the rhetoric of Jas 4. James chides the readers for letting their desires and passions create divisions in the community (4:1–3). He then equates "friendship with the world" and "enmity with God" (4:4), provides evidence from Scripture that envy and pride are not the ways in which God wishes people to walk (4:5–6), and closes with ten imperatives stressing the need for repentance.

Nowhere in this passage does friendship with God function as a reminder of God's provision. Rather, the language of friendship is used as

88. Batten, "Patron or Benefactor?," 261. Batten bases some of her observation on Danker, "Bridging," 84–94.

89. See *Opif.* 169; *Leg.* 1:96, 2:56, 3:137; *Sacr.* 127; *Post.* 154; *Deus* 110; *Plant.* 87, 90; *Sobr.* 50, 58; *Congr.* 38, 97, 171; *Mut.* 28; *Somn.* 1:163; *Mos.* 2:256; *Decal.* 41; *Spec.* 1:152, 1:209, 1:221, 1:272, 1:300, 2:219; *Virt.* 41; *Legat.* 118.

90. Apart from Philo, as far as I know, the word εὐεργέτης is never used in Jewish writings for God. It is found seven times in LXX (including 3–4 Macc.) and thirty-six times in Josephus, always for human beings. It is never used in the known Greek pseudepigrapha. It is rare also in early Christian writings: the title is found only once (1 Clem 59:3) in the Apostolic Fathers, and only a few times in apocryphal literature (2x in Acts Pil. 9:2, Acts John 108:1 [of Jesus], Acts Phil. 35:2).

91. "The Gk. translations generally avoid the word group." Bertram, "Εὐεργετέω, Εὐεργέτης, Εὐεργεσία," 2:654. The nine verses referring to God are 2 Macc 6:13; 10:38; Ps 12:6; 56:3; 77:11; 114:7; Wis 3:5; 16:2; 16:11.

92. Only the *Letter of Aristeas* depicts God as a benefactor, but the three occurrences of the idea (*Let. Aris.* 190, 210, 281) stress the universal nature of God's benefaction, and so are useless to prove Batten's idea of God acting as a benefactor to a specific group of people.

an indictment of the double-minded (cf. 4:8). The vocative "adulteresses!" (μοιχαλίδες) in 4:4—and, more generally, the whole tone of the passage—makes perfect sense if the passage is James's climactic rebuke to those who do not take the covenant seriously. It would be rather surprising if one supposes, with Batten, that this section aims at encouraging people to trust in God for their practical needs. Furthermore, nothing in the context points to the direction Batten wants to take the metaphor of friendship. James 4 never warns that human benefactors are not to be trusted.[93] Instead, James rather points to the impossibility of pledging allegiance to God and to "the world" at the same time. One should also note that James never presents God as the friend of the community.[94] James's language ("whoever wants to be a friend of the world appoints himself as God's enemy") point to the impossibility of friendship with God if one lives by the values of the κόσμος. James is not reassuring the community by saying that they are friends of God, nor does he extol the benefits of being God's friend. Instead, he exhorts his readers to take all the necessary steps to *make friendship with God possible* by aligning themselves with God's will. Those who become friends with the world cut themselves off from that possibility.

For these reasons, Batten's proposal does not provide a convincing argument for the meaning of friendship with God in the letter of James. A closer look at the text is necessary to get a better grasp on what he means. The next section will show that James speaks of "friendship with God" in a way that is quite consistent with other Jewish authors of his time, and that this illuminates the whole epistle with a powerful metaphor that brings together many threads of James's thought.

Friendship with God in James

Now that we have cleared the path—friendship with God is *not* a euphemism for taking God as a divine patron—we can define it in positive terms. First, we observe that friendship with God is, in James as much as in Philo or Ben Sira, an ideal to tend toward. Nowhere does James present his readers as friends of God, nor does he claim the title for himself. Only Abraham

---

93. Even if one reads Jas 2:1–13 as an attack against patronage, as Batten does, there is no compelling reason to believe that this concern is still preponderant in chapter 4, or is a central theme of the letter. In any case, James gives no evidence that friendship with God is related to trusting God for one's practical needs. Moreover, as we have seen, this is not the way first-century Jews used the language of friendship with God.

94. We will discuss the importance of this in the next section.

is called God's friend in James's epistle (2:23). Moreover, James stresses that Abraham became God's friend only *at the end* of a lifetime of obedience. In short, friendship with God is not a status the community already possesses, but an ideal toward which each is called to move.

James 4:4 stresses that friendship with God cannot be developed unless "friendship with the world" is abandoned. Since the latter has to do especially with giving up evil desires (4:1–2), jealousy (4:5), and pride (4:6), one can become a friend of God only by giving up these things. Here, James comes close to Philo's comment that friends of God are free from vain glory, desires, and anger (*Sobr.* 57, *Prob.* 45). Moreover, as we will see later, many other passages in the letter invite the readers to emulate God's actions and character, something that makes perfect sense within the concept of friendship seen as a relationship based on sharing identical aspirations and worldviews.

Three features in Abraham's portrait stand out. First, Abraham's perfect faith is stressed. James highlights that Abraham's "faith worked together with his works" (συνεργέω, 2:22) so that his faith was "perfected" (τελειόω, 2:22). Hence, Abraham also provides an example of the perfection, or wholeness, James wants his readers to attain (see 1:2–4, 12). The element of faith is particularly significant in view of our discussion of "the world" in the last chapter. We saw that "the world" stands for a worldview that does not take God or his promises into account. Johnson points out that Abraham became a friend of God because he accepted "God's way of seeing the situation and acted on it. According to the measure of 'the world,' the sacrifice of his own beloved son would have been senseless. . . . If Abraham had seen things the way 'the world' did—a measure of reality, we remember, which excludes God's claim—he would have rejected God's call to obedience."[95] Hence, friendship with God is developed by acting in ways that demonstrate that God's "measure of reality" takes precedence over "the measure of 'the world'"—that is, by acting by faith.

In inviting his readers to develop friendship with God rather than with the κόσμος, James highlights the need to take God and his promises with utter seriousness. This is possible only through faith. Hence, being a friend of God is grounded, first and foremost, in a deep trust in God's generosity. James's God is the giving Father who gives to his children what they need (1:5, 17, 21; 5:15), especially wisdom (1:5) and salvation (1:21). Faith implies both humility—the recognition that every human being needs God's

---

95. Johnson, "Friendship," 215.

FRIENDSHIP OR ENMITY?

help—and confidence that God's character is such that his help is readily available to anyone who asks. Friendship with God can only grow when God's faithful, merciful, and generous character is recognized.

Second, the mention of the binding of Isaac (*Akedah*) in 2:21 probably functions, at least in part, as a reminder of the ten trials of Abraham.[96] The *Akedah* was the last, "the greatest (*Jub.* 17:16; Philo, *Abr.* 167), the most difficult and the most important of the 'tests' to which God subjected Abraham to prove his faithfulness and obedience."[97] Hence, James agrees with Ben Sira that friendship with God presupposes steadfastness in times of trial.[98] The ideas of perfection and of trials both belong to the notion of a process over time that finds its climax in friendship. This element of progress provides a powerful element of encouragement to believers going through a time of ordeal. They can be assured that trials have a τέλος (5:11), a word with a double connotation. First, suffering has an end. It will not go on forever (5:7–8, 11, 15). Second and more importantly, suffering—although itself an evil to be mourned and countered when possible—has a positive outcome (1:2–4, 12; 5:11). Through faith, trials can be accepted with joy (1:2) because of the incomparable value of their outcome both in this life (1:4) and in the next (1:12).

Third, Abraham is also a model of single-minded devotion to God. Most often, the *Akedah* serves as a demonstration that Abraham mastered his affections, that his love for God was stronger than his love for his family.[99] Jacobs shows that other developments on the *Akedah*, more or less contemporary to James, stress the idea that Abraham did obey God's command rather than his own desires, even though the desire to protect his son was more than legitimate.[100] James then refers to this episode of Abraham's life as an indirect call to place God above everything else, even one's family.[101] Gerd Theissen suggests that Abraham and Rahab were tied

---

96. On the tradition of the ten trials, see Milgrom, *Binding of Isaac*, 34–62; Allison, *James*, 488.

97. Bauckham, "James, 1 and 2 Peter, Jude," 306.

98. The importance of trials of faith is evident in Jas 1:2–4, 12, 13–16.

99. See Wis. 10:5; *L.A.B.* 18:5, 32:2–4; 4 Macc 14:20; Philo *Abr.* 170, 198, *Virt.* 218, *Deus.* 4; Josephus *A.J.* 1.13.1 §222–24; *Gen. Rab.* 55:7, 56:4, 56:8, 56:10; Origen *Hom. Gen.* 8:2.

100. Jacobs, "Midrashic Background," 461.

101. The theme of loyalty to God taking precedence over familial obligations and loyalty is also prominent in Jesus's teaching. Cf. Matt 8:21–22; 10:34–38; 12:46–50; 19:29; 23:8–10, and parallels.

together by the fact that both characters placed faithfulness to God above other commitments—Abraham to his family and Rahab to her citizenship.[102] Since family and cities were the two main spheres through which identity was derived in the first century, Theissen proposes that the examples of Abraham and Rahab imply more than putting one's faith into practice: these examples also imply the willingness to let one's faith define one's identity, even when doing so entails separation from one's family or one's *polis*. Single-mindedness, therefore, includes more than rejecting idolatry, or "friendship with the world." It also implies letting God take precedence over any other consideration.

Therefore, using the language of friendship with God and referring to Abraham enabled James to tie together the essential points of his epistle—perfection, steadfastness in trials, and single-mindedness—with a single concept.

CONCLUSION

In the course of this chapter, we have seen that "friendship with the world" is a complete alignment with the value system that exalts envy, self-assertion, and destructive speech. James insists that the set of values on which human society is grounded—along with its institutions and everything it produces—is a corrupt system that must be utterly rejected. We concluded that refusing to become a "friend of the world" simply means hatred of evil—that is, the absolute commitment to reject everything that hinders love for God (the Shema alluded to in 2:19 and 4:12) and for one's neighbor (2:8). Not being "friends of the world" thus brings the people together as a united community. Crucially, however, James never encourages his readers to adopt a sectarian stance. The opposite expression, "friendship with God," is defined as a complete adherence to the virtues of God, to the point that God's qualities end up being impressed on the character of his friends. This implies that friendship with God functions as an ideal toward which to strive.

This raises a few important questions. Since the worldview on which human society rests is so hopelessly corrupted, is hope for society even possible? Does James's community have a positive role to play for the larger society? Is the community invited to care for the poor only within its own boundaries, or also beyond those boundaries? We will now turn to these questions.

102. Theissen, "Éthique et communauté," 176.

4

The Role of the Church in the Letter of James

INTRODUCTION

THE PREVIOUS CHAPTERS DEFINED "the world" and "friendship with the world" in the context of James's epistle. It has become clear that the word κόσμος is never used to refer to a spacial reality (the universe, the earth, etc.) or of human society in general. Rather, it is consistently used to refer to a value system that is closed in on itself, shutting itself off from God and his kingdom. Consequently, the rejection of the κόσμος cannot be understood as a denial of the goodness of the created order. Nothing in James points towards that direction. Rather, rejecting the friendship of the world is the refusal to associate oneself with evil in all of its forms, even—or especially—in its socially acceptable forms. In short, rejecting "friendship with the world" speaks about the call to dissociate oneself from society *in all the domains in which that society embraces evil and rejects God's royal law.*

If this restricts our options in understanding the kind of relationship James sees between the believer and human society—and the relationship between the church and society—it does not yet make that relationship clear. As we have seen, James condemns in the strongest terms some of the attitudes characteristic of the culture he finds himself in—especially on topics such as wealth, honor, and language—but it is not yet clear whether the believer is granted a positive role in human society or not. In order to understand the way James holds in tension the rejection of the κόσμος—i.e., the worldview of the society in which he lives—*and* the continued presence of the Christian within that society, we must now study the role James grants to the church, and to individual Christians, within society.

Unfortunately for us, James never specifies his understanding of the mission, or purpose, of the church.[1] As Andrew Chester succinctly puts it: "James has no developed ecclesiology."[2] His imperatives are of a general nature, and themes such as evangelism or the nature of the church are never developed in the epistle. The absence of an invitation to proclaim the gospel is a striking feature of James's letter. If we are to believe the book of Acts, evangelism has been an important element of the Christian movement from its inception. Therefore, James's unmistakable focus on the community will have to be accounted for, especially since we cannot simply write it off as a corollary of a sectarian stance.

One should not deduce too quickly from James's silence, however, that there is "no evidence of any thrust amounting to a proclaiming of the Good News about the present."[3] First, James is a short book, and we cannot assume that it presents a comprehensive teaching.[4] James aims at shaping the concrete behavior of the Christian, at fortifying the existing community, and at restoring a proper perspective where it has gone awry. The fact that he is silent on many topics cannot be taken as a sign that he regards them as unimportant. The interest James takes in the community choosing good teachers suggests that he grants teachers an essential role in shaping the Christian community. Their task probably includes educating the community on the topics he is not able to develop in his letter. Second, it is also quite likely that James does not proclaim the message of salvation because he assumes it. His letter is not evangelistic in nature; his concern is not to explain the basics of faith, but to make sure that believers let their faith shape the whole of their life.[5] Just as it seems likely that James is silent on

---

1. This, no doubt, is the reason why this theme is only rarely developed in scholarship. To my knowledge, the only scholars who addressed this question in some length are Richard Bauckham and William Baker. See Bauckham, "James, 1 Peter," 153–66; Baker, "Community," 208–25.

2. Chester and Martin, *Theology*, 41.

3. Witherington, *Jesus the Sage*, 245.

4. Davids makes the same point: "in James, therefore, we are evidently dealing with only a small portion of an author's thought and values." Davids, "Controlling the Tongue," 226.

5. See Polhill, "Prejudice," 395.

many topics usually discussed in wisdom literature—like familial relationships or sexual ethics—because he assumes his audience would agree with him, he probably avoids speaking about ecclesiology and mission simply because he assumes that his readers will share his perspective.

As a consequence, we are left to read between the lines, as it were, to discern what James's teaching on mission and ecclesiology would be. This task is not entirely hopeless, however, because James gives us some hints that can help us to reconstruct the main elements of his ecclesiology and sense of mission. In what follows, I will gather these hints in the hope of creating a comprehensive picture on these topics. I propose that a close reading of James reveals three elements: the community is called to be (1) the *foretaste* of God's kingdom, (2) a *sign* that this kingdom will indeed prevail, and (3) an *instrument* of God for the redemption of creation.

THE COMMUNITY AS A FORETASTE OF GOD'S KINGDOM

James speaks of Torah as the "law of liberty" (Jas 1:25; 2:12) and the "royal law." As we saw in Chapter 1, these qualifications indicate that believers have been set free to serve God in a renewed way, and that they live according to the rules of God's kingdom. As Konradt puts it, to specify that the law is *royal* "implies that it defines the life order of the kingdom given by God as the king, which is already binding in this world with its different social order for those who wish to inherit the kingdom."[6] Hence, God's law shapes the readers into a different community that already embodies, in the here and now, the eschatological community. "Faithfulness and obedience to God's law breaks down the wall between the kingdom of heaven and earth, and the eschatological blessing is proleptically found *in the actual doing*. As his people act in accordance with the Wisdom and Law of the kingdom, so they find themselves living in the blessings of the kingdom *now*."[7]

James also invites the members of the congregation to let themselves be shaped by God's wisdom and character (3:17; cf. 1:17). The simple fact of presenting friendship with God as an (attainable) ideal implies that the readers will strive to have their characters, actions, and desires formed after God's. For James, God's character represents what Christians are called to emulate. Examples of the *imitatio Dei* abound in the letter. Believers are

---

6. Konradt, "Love Command," 280.
7. Kovalishyn, "Apocalyptic Wisdom," 304 (emphasis original).

called to be single-minded (1:8), just as God himself gives with simplicity (ἁπλῶς). They are called to take care of the orphans and widows (1:27; 2:14-16), which is the classical biblical example of imitating God (cf. Deut 10:17-18).[8] The community is to show mercy because *God is merciful*.[9] As Hartin neatly summarizes, "the imitation of God is not expressed directly, but it certainly operates in an indirect way."[10]

The "royal law" (2:8) and the "wisdom from above" (3:17) thus provide the community with its proper structure and distinctive outlook. James's community is fashioned by the glory of Christ and a sense of honor antithetical to a worldly definition of honor. Instead of a society organized around money and the honor derived from money, it promotes an ordering of society in which wealth is irrelevant. Within this society, the poor are respected and honored (2:5), and the rich must agree to relinquish any advantage due to their wealth—they are to be treated like everyone else. Moreover, material goods are measured by the way they are used to care for those in need (4:17). In these broad strokes, James depicts an ideal society whose realization would imply a radical reshaping of the established social order.[11] Establishing a foretaste of God's kingdom on earth plays a double role: it offers non-believers a demonstration of God's wisdom, and creates a space in which the oppressed find relief.

The Community as a Demonstration of God's Wisdom

The wisdom of God is best demonstrated when the Christian community lives out God's commands and so experiences peaceful relationships and flourishing life. For James, the church is a "model community" that embodies the wisdom from above and so proves the superiority of God's wisdom to the κόσμος. Like almost everything in James's ecclesiology, this remains implicit, but two things make it almost certain that James intended this goal.

First, the idea that the way of life of Jesus's followers leads non-believers to acknowledge God's glory is central to Jesus's message as presented in

---

8. On the centrality of Deut 10:17-18 for the theme of *imitatio Dei*, see Barton, "Imitation," 36.

9. For a longer discussion on the imitation of God in James, see Hartin, *Spirituality of Perfection*, 100-01, 140-44; Cheung, *Genre*, 104-21.

10. Hartin, *Spirituality of Perfection*, 142.

11. For a fuller description of this reshaping, see Konradt, "Love Command," 279-81.

the Sermon on the Mount (see especially Matt 5:14–16). Given the number of similarities between James and the Sermon, it is quite natural to assume that James shares Jesus's motivation on this point.[12] Moreover, peaceful relationships were often seen as the means *par excellence* to show God's presence.[13] "Nothing expresses kingdom realities more than reconciled relations."[14] Given James's constant focus on healthy communal relationships, it is not unlikely that he has this in mind as well.

Second, the pericope on the wisdom from above (3:13–18) points in the same direction. The call to *show* (δείκνυμι) one's wisdom in Jas 3:13 is grounded on one of the clearest OT passages in which Israel's obedience leads it to be a demonstration of God's goodness. The rhetorical question opening James's paragraph ("Who is wise and understanding among you; Τίς σοφὸς καὶ ἐπιστήμων ἐν ὑμῖν;") reminds the reader of Deut 4:6–8.[15] These verses are not taken from a random passage from Torah but from *the* pericope equating Torah to wisdom: "the words of Moses in Deut 4 . . . embody the basic message of the Pentateuch as a whole. Wisdom comes from knowing and obeying the written word of God, the Torah."[16] Deuteronomy 4:6–8 speaks explicitly of Israel displaying God's wisdom "in the sight of the nations" (MT: לְעֵינֵי הָעַמִּים; LXX: ἐναντίον πάντων τῶν ἐθνῶν). Hence, "obedience to the law was not for Israel's benefit alone. It is a marked feature of the Old Testament that Israel lived on a very public stage."[17] By alluding to this text, James transfers the role of being witnesses of God's wisdom from the nation of Israel to the community he addresses.

---

12. See especially Hartin, "Q Sermon," 440–57; Wick, "You Shall Not Murder," 88–96; Porter, "Sermon on the Mount, Part 1," 344–60; Porter, "Sermon on the Mount, Part 2," 470–82. On Jas 3:13–18 and Matt 5–8, see also McKnight, *James*, 147–48.

13. Cf. esp. John 13:35; 17:21; Acts 4:32–35; 5:12–13.

14. Scot McKnight, *Sermon on the Mount*, 82.

15. Beside Deut 4:6, σοφὸς and ἐπιστήμων are only found together (in the LXX) in Deut 1:13 and 1:15, which speak of the quality required for the leaders of Israel appointed by Moses in the desert. The same adjectives also appear in Dan 1:4; 5:11 and Sir 10:25; 21:15, but not in the same configuration. The interrogative form also suggests a link with LXX Hosea 14:10 that uses similar vocabulary. Karen Jobes argues that this is the text James has in mind, but also recognizes the closeness to Deut 4:6. She writes, "if James has Deut. 4.6 in mind, he is thinking of it as mediated through the message of Hosea." See Jobes, "Minor Prophets," 138. She is followed by Allison, *James*, 569. For our present purpose, however, the echo of Deuteronomy is more important than the one of Hosea.

16. Sailhamer, "Wisdom Composition," 28.

17. Wright, *Mission of God*, 378.

Two elements strengthen the suggestion that James applies this text to his audience. First, Deut 4:6–8 speaks of Israel's "greatness" somewhat ironically, well aware that Israel is actually a small nation (cf. Deut 7:7). Greatness is redefined in terms of the "righteousness" (4:8; MT: צַדִּיק; LXX: δίκαιος) of the law that stresses "the nearness of the living God in prayer and the social justice of [Israel's] constitution and laws," two central themes of James's theology.[18] Second, the view of Torah found in Jewish sapiential texts written from the second and first century BCE is drawn in large part from Deut 4:6–8. Independent arguments have been offered that these verses plays a major role in the view of Torah advanced in the books of Ben Sira, the letter of Baruch, and the *letter of Aristeas*.[19] These at least demonstrate that Deut 4:6–8 was well known and quite influential among wisdom teachers. It is therefore reasonable that this text played an important role in James's understanding of wisdom.

The Community as a Place of Blessing

In addition to being a model community, James's audience is called to bless the poor in concrete ways. The members of the community embody, in the present world, the future kingdom in which these values will be fully realized. By living according to the "wisdom from above" and the "royal law," followers of Jesus create on earth below an enclave of the kingdom of above. In Bauckham's words, the community "pioneers the life of God's coming kingdom."[20] This is nowhere as visible as in the eschatological reversal that is already inaugurated in the community (Jas 1:9–11; 2:5). The poor, both inside and outside of the community, are blessed through the existence of the church.

Blessing the Poor within the Community

The community *is* good news to the poor, primarily in two ways. First, it provides partial relief from their plight. The poor find in the community a place where they are genuinely appreciated, honored and cared for. This is

---

18. Wright, *Mission of God*, 379n20.

19. For Ben Sira, see Gilbert, "Wisdom Literature," 295. For Baruch, see Hogan, "Elusive Wisdom," 158. For the *Letter of Aristeas*, see Matusova, *Meaning*, 37. For the influence of Deut 4:6–8 on other sapiential texts of that period, see also Marttila and Pajunen, "Wisdom," 2–26.

20. Bauckham, *James*, 100.

obvious from Jas 1:27 and the whole of chapter 2, and it has been discussed at length already. There is, however, another aspect of the honor due the poor which has not yet been underlined: the strict equality of value among all human beings.

First of all, since the community is already organized according to the values of God's kingdom, the poor are treated as enjoying equal status with everyone else. Moreover, Jas 3:9 stresses that all human beings are created in God's image and, therefore, have equal value.[21] The fact that James addresses his readers as "brothers"—never placing himself above his audience, but presenting himself as one of them—further supports the same idea. Johnson notes that "ancient wisdom massively reinforced a stratified view of the world in which the older had more authority than the younger, the free more than slaves, men more than women, the rich more than the poor. James decisively rejects that view of the world."[22] Hence, "James is egalitarian rather than hierarchical."[23] Finally, the examples chosen throughout the letter also point in that direction: "Abraham our father" (2:21) and "Rahab the prostitute" (2:25) are cited side by side, suggesting that their examples hold the same authority. The description of Elijah as "a man having the same nature as us" (ἄνθρωπος ὁμοιοπαθὴς ἡμῖν, Jas 5:17) contrasts with the usual description of an almost superhuman figure.[24] All these elements point toward a desire to create a community in which the distinctions that prevail outside of it are set aside. For James, "true faith excludes the making of social distinctions."[25]

Blessing the Poor Outside of the Community

In James's view, the community should not be content to bless only those who belong to it. Three passages are especially informative in this regard.

---

21. The allusion to Gen 1:26 indicates that Jas 3:9 applies to the dignity of any human being, irrespective of its gender, ethnicity, or social status. Such an honor is due to everyone, whether or not they are part of the community. The force with which James forbids double-talk in 3:10 (οὐ χρή, "this should absolutely not be") indicates how strongly James feels about this. Χρή is a hapax in the NT and appears only once in the LXX. Biblical authors almost exclusively use δεῖ. In classical Greek, χρή is common and stronger than δεῖ. See Assaël and Cuvillier, *Epître de Saint-Jacques*, 217.

22. Johnson, *Brother of Jesus*, 28.

23. Johnson, *Brother of Jesus*, 28.

24. See the discussion in Davids, "Tradition," 120–21; Wall, *Community*, 270.

25. Hartin, "The Poor," 149.

James 2:14-16

The section on the topic of faith and works (2:14-26) implies that believers are called help the poor in concrete ways (2:15-16). These verses speak about of helping "*a brother or a sister*" (ἐὰν ἀδελφὸς ἢ ἀδελφὴ γυμνοὶ ὑπάρχωσιν . . . , v. 15)—that is, someone who belongs to the community.[26] And yet, two elements intimate that the invitation to provide the poor with life's most basic necessities should be extended to the poor outside the community. First, 2:14-26 continues the train of thought begun in 2:1-13, which speaks about two men, obviously not known, visiting the church (2:2-4). James 2:14-16 functions as a commentary on what the *mercy* spoken of in 2:13 (κατακαυχᾶται ἔλεος κρίσεως, "mercy triumphs over [eschatological] judgment") looks like in practice, which suggests that the poor visitor of 2:2 is still in view. Second, the duty to help the poor is never restricted to Israel's poor in the OT, nor to the Christian community in the NT. When a distinction is made, it is only one of degree or priority; Scripture offers a unanimous witness that the needy are to be cared for whatever their background may be. Given the emphasis on this topic in the letter of James, particularly the consistent call to be merciful to the alien in their midst, it is unthinkable that this would not be the case here.

James 3:10-12

The image in Jas 3:10-12 of a source (or well, πηγή, v. 11) that cannot bring both fresh and salty water serves primarily as a rebuke of hypocrisy: speech in the community should be as invigorating as fresh water and should not produce bitterness (cf. 3:14ff). Nevertheless, the term πηγή is so loaded in biblical imagery that it invites the reader to go beyond the literal meaning of the phrase and meditate on it. In wisdom texts, wise words are often identified as "a source of life" (πηγὴ ζωῆς).[27] Similar images also appear in the Psalms (36:9 [LXX 35:10]; 42:1 [41:2]; 68:26 [67:27]) and prophetic literature. In the latter, the same word is taken up as a metaphor for God himself (Jer 2:13; 17:13), or functions as an image of eschatological restoration (Joel 3:18; Is 12:3, 35:7; 49:10; 58:11). Inasmuch as these ideas are frequent in the OT, they would easily be associated with the word πηγή.

---

26. McKnight (*Letter of James*, 230n19) also notes we can assume that James thinks believers should help the poor outside of the community, even if this is not what is at issue here.

27. See LXX Pr. 6:11; 10:11; 13:14; 14:27; 16:22; 18:4; Sir 21:13.

Hence, James invites his readers to meditate on the ways they can become this fountain of life.[28] Just as cursing—which corresponds to bitter water—is forbidden on the ground that every human being is made in the image of God (vv. 9–10), the fresh water of blessing meant to flow towards the whole humanity. The words of wisdom treasured and cultivated in the community are to overflow and bring life wherever those who have received wisdom from above find themselves.

James 4:13–17

James concludes his indictment of the arrogant merchant in 4:13–17 with a proverbial statement: "So whoever knows the right thing to do and fails to do it, for him it is sin" (4:17, following the ESV; εἰδότι οὖν καλὸν ποιεῖν καὶ μὴ ποιοῦντι, ἁμαρτία αὐτῷ ἐστιν.). The verse seems rather unconnected to its context when translated this way, and some commentators assume that James clumsily integrates a known proverb in the section.[29] However, when the participle εἰδότι is understood not with a cognitive nuance but with the connotation of capacity, the sentence makes perfect sense in its context.[30] James is rebuking merchants who are not doing the good they are *able* to do.

Two elements point to this reading. First, Jas 4:11–5:6 is best understood as the second half of a section that expands the phrase "God opposes the proud but gives greater grace to the humble" (Prov 3:34), cited in Jas 4:6. After issuing a call to humility (4:7–10), James exposes three types of increasingly prideful behavior (4:11–12, 13–17; 5:1–6).[31] Since Jas 4:13–17 develops the thought of Prov 3:34, it is reasonable to think that James intends his readers to hear an allusion to Prov 3:27–28 in these verses.[32] The words are different, but the ideas are identical.[33]

28. Allison (*James*, 556) has an interesting note here: "Dibelius, 203, protests that this sort of reading [i.e. forms of allegorical reading] is 'superfluous'. He is strictly speaking correct, but the text invites it nonetheless."

29. Allison (*James*, 663) lists a number of commentators who take that view.

30. Cf. BDAG s.v. οἶδα, §3.

31. That these three sections are to be understood as a development of 4:6 is indicated by the repetition of the verb ἀντιτάσσω (4:6; 5:6) that create an inclusio. See Schökel, "James 5:2 [sic]," 73–76; followed by Johnson, *Letter of James: A New Translation*, 292.

32. Laws believes that a connection between the two texts is "quite possible." See Laws, *James*, 194. For other parallels between Jas 4 and Prov 3, see Allison, *James*, 624.

33. The last part of verse 28 is not found in the MT. It seems to be added from Prov 27:1, with the transformation of γινώσκεις into οἶδας. Prov 27:1 prevents boasting about

James 4:17	Proverbs 3:27–28
Therefore, to anyone able to do good but not doing it, it is sin for him.	Do not refrain from doing good to the poor, when your hand can help.
	Do not say: ". . . tomorrow I will give" when you are able to do good.
James 4:14	
You who do not know what will happen tomorrow. . .	For you do not know what the next day will bring.
εἰδότι οὖν καλὸν ποιεῖν καὶ μὴ ποιοῦντι, ἁμαρτία αὐτῷ ἐστιν.	μὴ ἀπόσχῃ εὖ ποιεῖν ἐνδεῆ, ἡνίκα ἂν ἔχῃ ἡ χείρ σου βοηθεῖν· μὴ εἴπῃς . . . αὔριον δώσω, δυνατοῦ σου ὄντος εὖ ποιεῖν·
οἵτινες οὐκ ἐπίστασθε τὸ τῆς αὔριον. . .	οὐ γὰρ οἶδας τί τέξεται ἡ ἐπιοῦσα.

If there is a link between these passages, then the rebuke in 4:17 concerns those who could give alms but do not. "The actions of the merchants are condemned partially because they 'are directed solely to the attainment of more and more wealth'" (cf. 4:13, which ends with the statement "we will make profit"—κερδαίνω).³⁴ This interpretation is further supported by the use of καλὸν ποιεῖν instead of καλῶς ποιεῖν (as in 2:8, 19). The adverb—with the connotation "to do well"—would be more typical than the adjective, "but the use of the noun in the phrase *to do good* (*kalon poiein*) indicates that it is rather deed of goodness that are here in mind."³⁵ Moreover, the use of ποιέω also reminds the reader of the importance to put the word into practice (1:21–25; 2:14–26).

Another interesting parallel is found in the *Testament of Job*, an apocryphal book that many believe James knew.³⁶ In that book, Job gives his

---

the next day, and Bauckham considers that this text "certainly lies in the background" of Jas 4:13–14. See Bauckham, "Relevance," 99.

34. Garrett, "Message to the Merchants," 232.

35. Laws, *Commentary*, 193. Davids agrees and cites the parallel with "charitable deeds" in Gal 6:9 (*Epistle of James*, 174).

36. The longest argument for James's dependence on the Testament of Job has been offered in deSilva, *Jewish Teachers*, 237–51. DeSilva's main arguments are the following. First, there is a cluster of common themes and vocabulary between *T. Job* and Jas 5:7–11.

children an account of all that he did for the destitute. The account specifies that others were prompted by Job's example and used to come to him, asking loans in order to build trading posts in other cities for the purpose of helping the poor with the benefits (*T. Job* 11).[37] The wording of their request is not far from the imagined thoughts of the merchants in James 4:13.

James 4:13	*T. Job* 11:3
We will go into such and such city,	. . . so that we may go in this city far-away,
and we will spend a year there,	
and we will do business,	and [so that], by doing business,
and we will make a profit.	we may be able to do a service to the poor.
πορευσόμεθα εἰς τήνδε τὴν πόλιν	. . . ἵνα ἀπέλθωμεν εἰς τὰς μακρὰς πόλεις
καὶ ποιήσομεν ἐκεῖ ἐνιαυτὸν	
καὶ ἐμπορευσόμεθα	καὶ ἐμπορευόμενοι
καὶ κερδήσομεν.	τοῖς πένησιν δυνηθῶμεν ποιήσασθαι διακονίαν·

The similarity in wording does not suffice to demonstrate borrowing on James's part, but since it is argued on other grounds that James was familiar with that document, the similarity is striking, especially given the fact that ἐμπορεύομαι is a fairly rare verb.[38] The place where the parallel breaks between the texts comes at the end of the speech, the part that reveals the motivation of each protagonist. Hence, after reproving the merchants for leading their business without reference to God's desires (v. 15), James now

---

Second, the canonical Job does not fit James's picture of a paragon of endurance, which is precisely one of the main themes of *T. Job*. Patrick Gray provides even more thematic parallels between *T. Job* and the epistle of James, but concludes that, despite "impressive family resemblance" between the two texts, it is not possible "to prove beyond all doubt" that James borrowed from *T. Job*. Gray, "Points and Lines," 422. See also Davids, *Epistle of James*, 187–88.

37. Allison thinks that reading Jas 4:13–17 with this parallel in mind makes best sense of v. 17 within its context. Gray also notes this parallel. Allison, *James*, 665; Gray, "Points and Lines," 414n29.

38. It occurs only twice in the NT, eleven times in LXX, five times in Philo, three times in Josephus, three times in Greek Pseudepigrapha, and not at all never in the apocryphal Gospels, Acts, or Apocalypses.

claims that the proper goal of business is to offer one's profit—at least part of it—for the benefit of the poor.[39]

James 4:13–17, then, is more than a mere condemnation of arrogance. James does not oppose business as such, but he does proscribe business conducted for the sole purpose of making money. For him, the only acceptable aim for doing business is to multiply one's resources so as to multiply one's ability to provide for those in need.

THE COMMUNITY AS A WARNING TO THE ΚΌΣΜΟΣ

We have seen that the role of being a foretaste of God's kingdom contains two elements: demonstrating God's wisdom to "the world" and offering the poor a place in which they can find rest and relief. In addition to this role, which one could call the constructive side of the community's task, James also lays upon the community a more challenging responsibility—namely, to perform an admonitory function.

First, the epistle contains various warnings to the rich, demonstrating the spiritual danger associated with wealth in James's mind.[40] Even though it is a dominant theme of the letter, two caveats needs to be made. The first is that the clearest denunciation of the rich (5:1–6) is patterned after the OT prophetic indictment and, therefore, is probably addressed to the poor rather than to the rich.[41] These verses are meant primarily to reassure the oppressed—by affirming that justice would be done—rather than to warn the rich. In short, the rich may never have heard James's words of condemnation. The other caveat is that the denunciation of wealth is not a direct responsibility of the community.[42] James never invites them to oppose the rich in an active way.

---

39. Other Jewish texts also express the idea that giving up covetousness is not sufficient in itself but should be followed by a practice of sharing what one has with the poor. See, for instance, *T. Benj.* 5:1.

40. See especially 1:10–11; 5:1–6; cf. 2:5–7; 4:14. For a full study on the topic, see Maynard-Reid, *Poverty*. See also Hartin, "The Poor."

41. This is a fairly common interpretation of these words. See Maynard-Reid, *Poverty*, 81; Stulac, *James*, 162–63; Blomberg and Kamell, *James*, 206; Moo, *James*, 164; Vlachos, *James*, 184; Martin, *James*, 172–73.

42. At the same time, one could argue that the way the community treats the rich (if it follows James's advice in 2:1–13) is already a kind prophetic warning, in that the egalitarian treatment of the rich manifests the proper way to interact with wealthier people. However, it would only be a side point to this pericope.

Yet, even with these caveats in mind, James's words against the rich still point to the fact that the community is shaped by an ethos of uncompromising opposition to oppressive behaviors typical of the κόσμος. The tone of these passages also suggests that the community is not—or at least should not be—afraid to manifest its disapproval of oppression. Since James condemns it in such unambiguous terms, he would certainly approve of other teachers doing the same. Hence, even though the denunciation of oppression is not a burden laid on the community (the community is never invited to take a revolutionary stance—indeed, quite the contrary), its teachers are nonetheless called to remind worshippers that their faith is irreconcilable with the unjust treatment of the poor.

The section on patience in Jas 5:7–11—a section that rests upon an eschatological perspective that is taken for granted—also points to the fact that the community stands as a warning to the κόσμος.[43] The audience is exhorted to be patient (μακροθυμία, 5:7, 8, 10) and to emulate Job's endurance (ὑπομονή, 5:11) in times of trials. Each of these nouns highlights one aspect of the attitude necessary to the community. It must first be patient in its expectation for the eschatological reversal, living faithfully until its arrival.[44] The images of the farmer waiting for the fruit of the earth (5:7), of the parousia of the Lord (5:8), and of the judge standing at the door (5:9) further stress the necessity of patience while, at the same time, encouraging the audience to see the eschaton as imminent.

The idea that the community stands as a warning sign to the κόσμος emerges from the virtue of endurance James exhorts his audience to develop. Endurance is not, as sometimes supposed, a passive quality, but an active one.[45] Elza Tamez calls it "a militant, indomitable patience."[46] The examples that James uses—the prophets, Job, and Elijah—help us flesh out his understanding of endurance.

---

43. Expressions like παρουσία τοῦ κυρίου (vv. 7, 8) and ὁ κριτὴς πρὸ τῶν θυρῶν ἕστηκεν (v. 9) are typical of an eschatological setting, as is the theme of judgment (vv. 9, 12). The words chosen in the pericope on healing (σώζω, ἐγείρω, Jas 5:15) convey the same kind of connotation and functions as a double entendre. "The prayer of faith will save the sick one and the Lord will raise him up" can either indicate physical healing or salvation and resurrection. The phrase σώσει ψυχὴν αὐτοῦ refers to eternal salvation.

44. The verb στηρίζω ("establish your heart" in 5:8) is often used in eschatological context (see 1 Thess 3:13; 2 Thess 3:3; 1 Pet 5:10; Rev 3:2) and is typically associated with faithfulness. See Spicq, "Στηρίζω," 3:291–95.

45. See BDAG, s.v. ὑπομονή, §1.

46. Tamez, *Scandalous Message*, 46. Tamez discusses the topic on pp. 43–46.

The prophets "who spoke in the name of the Lord" (οἳ ἐλάλησαν ἐν τῷ ὀνόματι κυρίου, v.10) remind the reader that God's spokespersons are often rejected by their generation. These prophets suffered *because of* their determination to proclaim God's word to an unfaithful people. For James, "the prophets *spoke* the word of God faithfully into a hostile situation, and because of that, they had to *endure* the hostile world's response. They are not a model of passive suffering, but of active boldness pronouncing a different reality from the one we see."[47] The same is true for the people addressed in Jas 5:7–11. The first generations of Christians did not hesitate to count themselves as heirs to the prophetic tradition, and this is precisely what James does as well.[48] Because the community proclaims God's word—either in words or by embodying the message—it must be prepared not to give way even if its members face rejection, intimidation attempts, or physical violence because of their faithfulness.

The figure of Job stresses the same virtue. As noted above, James most likely refers to Job as portrayed in the *Testament of Job*, which takes endurance in trials as one of its central themes.[49] It is noteworthy that Job enters willingly into hardship: in this story, Job decides to oppose idol worship by destroying a temple, knowing what it would cost him.[50] Job's suffering, therefore, also comes from his commitment to single-minded worship of God in the midst of an idolatrous society. In light of James's equation of "friendship with the world" with idolatry in 4:4 and his definition of pure worship—which entails caring for the orphans and widows—in 1:26–27, one can deduce that James sees proper worship as a denunciation of the pursuit of wealth and honor typical of the κόσμος. The ways of "the world" can therefore be condemned through other means than words: living according to the values of God's kingdom is already an implicit condemnation of the pursuit of wealth. The community is invited to live, as Job did,

---

47. Kovalishyn, "Apocalyptic Wisdom," 302. See also Karris, "New Angles," 215.

48. The NT commonly associates the prophets and persecution. See Matt 5:12 (// Luke 6:22–26), Matt 23:29–39 (// Luke 11:46–52; 13:33–35); Acts 7:51–53; Rom 11:3–4; 1 Thess 2:14–16; Jas 5:10; Rev 11:17–18; 16:5–6; 18:21–19:2. Manton believes that the phrase "who spoke on the name of the Lord . . . denotes the cause of their sufferings." Manton, *James*, 316.

49. Job's first words in the book are: "I am your father Job, fully engaged in endurance" (ἐγὼ γάρ εἰμι ὁ πατὴρ ὑμῶν Ἰὼβ ἐν πάσῃ ὑπομονῇ γενόμενος). Job is said to have conquered Satan because of his endurance in 27:4. See also Gray, "Points and Lines," 412.

50. *T. Job* 4:3–5:2. James 4:4 equates accepting the values of "the world" with idolatry.

in light of another goal, another τέλος (Jas 5:11).⁵¹ Living in light of the eschaton implies seeing wealth as insignificant compared to mature faith (τέλειος καὶ ὁλόκληρος, 1:4), even though such faith must be developed through hardships (cf. Jas 1:2–4).⁵²

Third, the way James phrases his exhortation to pray in 5:16 can be taken as stressing the point that the community is to function as a warning to "the world." When James affirms that "the prayer *of a righteous person* is able to work great effect," (πολὺ ἰσχύει δέησις δικαίου ἐνεργουμένη), "the readers cannot but connect this to the charge against the rich in 5:6 that they had murdered *the righteous person*" (δίκαιος).⁵³ Through this textual link, James creates a connection between Elijah and righteous believers among the community. Since it is likely that James has the whole episode of Elijah in mind (cf. 1 Kgs 17–18), the conflict with the political powers (Ahab and Jezebel) may be in view here. According to Johnson, Elijah "was situated over against the powers of his world, as the oppressed poor are situated over against the rich."⁵⁴

Finally, one should note a significant difference between the OT prophets and James's community: the prophets were sent to the covenant people, whereas the community members serve as witnesses to everyone. The fact that James describes the community as "diaspora" (1:1) makes it likely that their neighbors were neither Jews nor Christians. Nonetheless, members of the community are invited to identify themselves with the OT prophets. Through its patient, persevering, and counter-cultural way of life, the community silently reminds "the world" that their God remains the righteous judge who opposes the proud (4:6) and the oppressors (5:6). The community's rejection of the κόσμος is manifested by its disdain for the pursuit of wealth and honors. This attitude brings to light the futility of such a pursuit and forces "the world" to reconsider its priorities.

---

51. In *T. Job*, the eschatological perspective relativizes the importance of wealth. See Gray, "Points and Lines," 413–20.

52. The terms τέλος and ὑπομονή create a connection between 5:11 and 1:2–4. See, for example, Martin, *James*, 195.

53. Johnson, *Letter of James*, 344 (emphasis mine).

54. Johnson, *Letter of James*, 344. More will be said later on the connections between Jas 5:7–11 and 5:13–18. As we will see, the connection highlighted here by Johnson rests on solid ground.

THE COMMUNITY AS GOD'S INSTRUMENT FOR THE RESTORATION OF CREATION

In addition to being good news for the poor and a warning to those who live according to the values of the κόσμος, the community is granted a third role, that of being instrumental to the restoration of creation. Two passages are central to this argument: Jas 1:18 and 5:7–18. Whereas many see in 1:18 an indication that James hopes for a more holistic redemption, the fact that 5:7–18 contains the same idea is more rarely acknowledged.

Community as First-Fruits of Creation

James 1:18 equates the Christian community with the "first-fruits of God's creatures."

> βουληθεὶς ἀπεκύησεν ἡμᾶς λόγῳ ἀληθείας εἰς τὸ εἶναι ἡμᾶς ἀπαρχήν τινα τῶν αὐτοῦ κτισμάτων.[55]
>
> Because he so willed it, God gave us birth by the word of truth so that we may be, in some sense, the first-fruits of his creatures.

Jews were quite familiar with the offering of first-fruits, as it was an important part of cultic regulations.[56] The image can take two different meanings: first-fruits represent both the best of the harvest (qualitative emphasis)—a portion entirely devoted to God—and the sign that the major part of the harvest is still to come (temporal emphasis). When the image is found in the NT, it usually stresses one of these elements, or occasionally both.[57] Most commentators of James defend a temporal understanding of the metaphor in this verse, usually because the phrase "the first-fruits *of his creatures*" (ἀπαρχήν … τῶν αὐτοῦ κτισμάτων) suggests that other creatures also belong to God.[58] Hence, James's audience is just the begin-

---

55. The only significant textual variant is to substitute ἑαυτοῦ for αὐτοῦ. This variant is defended by weighty witnesses such as ℵ², A, and C. This reading adds emphasis to the idea that the community is God's own special possession, but does not modify the general meaning of the verse.

56. See the Mishnah, *Bikkurim*, esp. *Bik.* 3.

57. Stressing the temporal aspect: Rom 8:23; 16:5; 1 Cor 15:20, 23; 16:15. Stressing the qualitative aspect: 2 Thess 2:3; Rev 14:4. Cf. 1 Clem 29:3, Philo, *Spec.*, 4:180. Containing both ideas: Rom 11:16.

58. Reading τῶν κτισμάτων as a partitive genitive. See Davids, *Epistle of James*, 90; Bauckham, *James*, 179; Cantinat, *Épîtres*, 79; McKnight, *James*, 130; Assaël and Cuvillier, *Epître de Saint-Jacques*, 180; Moo, *James*, 79–80.

ning of God's work of redemption. Some believe that James has in mind a greater number of people receiving new birth,[59] while others extend the scope of redemption to the whole creation.[60] In my view, the pervasiveness of creation language in the immediate context ("father of lights" in 1:17; birth language and "creatures" in 1:18) tips the balance in favor of the latter option, a position further supported by the fact that the word κτίσμα is never used for human beings in the LXX or NT.[61] In short, the metaphor of first-fruits points to a larger redemption of creation.

Deuteronomy 11:13-21 in James 5:7-18

In Jas 5:7 and 5:18, we find a similar idea expressed in the image of rain. These two verses are linked by a double mention of the "fruits of the earth" (5:7, τὸν τίμιον καρπὸν τῆς γῆς; 5:18, τὸν καρπὸν αὐτῆς [i.e., τῆς γῆς]) and are further related by borrowing from the same OT pericope: Deut 11:13-21.[62] Indeed, the expression πρόϊμος καὶ ὄψιμος [ὑετός] in 5:7 is taken from Deut 11:14,[63] and the phrase "the earth gave its fruit" (ἡ γῆ ἐβλάστησεν τὸν καρπὸν αὐτῆς) in 5:18 is the reversal of the curse found in Deut 11:17.[64]

| Deut 11:17 | ἡ γῆ | οὐ δώσει | τὸν καρπὸν αὐτῆς |
| Jas 5:18 | ἡ γῆ | ἐβλάστησεν | τὸν καρπὸν αὐτῆς |

If, as I propose, James does borrow from Deut 11:13-21, we should pay great attention to the significance of intertextuality, because the latter

59. Cantinat, Épîtres, 97; Assaël and Cuvillier, Epître de Saint-Jacques, 180; Hartin, "Who Is Wise," 983.

60. Davids, Epistle of James, 90; Bauckham, James, 179; McKnight, James, 130; Blomberg and Kamell, James, 76; Moo, James, 79-80; Ng, "Father-God Language," 48.

61. The word occurs six times in the LXX (3 Macc 5:11; Wis 9:2; 13:5; 14:11; Sir 36:14; 38:34) and four times in the NT (1 Tim 4:4; Jas 1:18; Rev 5:13; 8:9), but it never refers to human beings. The same is true for the Apostolic Fathers, where the word appears three times (Shep 17:2; 38:1; 47:3). Outside of biblical Greek, the word usually means "building" (e.g. Josephus, Wars 1.21.2, 7, 2.6.1). See LSJ s.v. κτίσις.

62. Few commentators notice the parallel, and even those who mention it often do not see it as particularly significant. Among notable exceptions, one can cite Johnson, Letter of James, 337; Reicke, Epistles, 61; McCartney, James, 241, 261.

63. Deuteronomy 11:14 reads: "he will give the early rain and the latter rain to you land in its season" (δώσει τὸν ὑετὸν τῇ γῇ σου καθ' ὥραν πρόϊμον καὶ ὄψιμον).

64. A stronger rationale for hearing an echo of Deut 11:13-21 in this text is offered in Appendix 1.

passage is nothing less than the second part of the Shema,[65] a passage faithful Jews probably already recited twice a day before 70 CE.[66]

Bo Reicke, one of the few scholars who comment on the link between 5:7 and 5:18, believes that the rain is a symbol of the saving grace of God.[67] That "the farmer awaiting the harvest is a familiar Jewish picture of salvation and the Last Judgment" underlines the same idea, and it is clear that the two verses function together as an invitation to pray for God's eschatological blessing.[68]

And yet, it seems quite probable that James has more in view than mere symbolism when he speaks of rain. The mention of the "early and late rain" in Deut 11:14 was already interpreted by the prophets as a promise related to the eschatological restoration of the land (see Joel 2:23; Hos 6:3; Zech 10:1).[69] This idea was further developed during the Second Temple Period, where the realm of eschatological blessing encompasses the whole earth,[70] and it seems likely that James follows the same stream of interpretation. The fact that the expression found in Deut 11:17 is transformed in Jas 5:17 through the replacement of the common verb δίδωμι by the uncommon one βλαστάνω (eight occurrences in LXX, four in the NT) points to that direction. James likely alludes to LXX Gen 1:11, where the verb is used for the first time, thus presenting the situation in a specific light: "it is as though the rain Elijah wrought restored the creation."[71] It is also possible—perhaps even more likely—that James echoes Joel 2:22–23, which speaks of the restoration of the land in language reminiscent of both Gen 1:11 and Deut

---

65. The prayer includes three different passages: Deut 6:4–9; 11:13–21; Num 15:37–41. Although it is not entirely clear when these texts were assembled, phylacteries found in Qumran show beyond doubt that Deut 6:4–9 and 11:13–21 were already read together in the first century. The date at which the Shema came to be recited in its final form is debated. For a list of these phylacteries, see Edgar, "Love-Command," 17n33. On the influence of the Shema and early Jewish liturgy in James's epistle, see Verseput, "James 1:17," 177–91.

66. When exactly the Shema began to be recited twice a day is debated, but there is no doubt that these texts were very well known before the destruction of the Temple. See Gribetz, "The Shema," 58–84. For more references, see also Verseput, "Morning Prayers," 197n7.

67. Reicke, *Epistles*, 61.

68. Adamson, *Epistle of James*, 191.

69. The other LXX passage in which the expression occurs (Jer 5:24) does not refer to eschatological blessing, but speaks of rain as a sign of God's faithfulness.

70. See Rev 21:16; *Haer.* 5.33.3; 2 Bar 29:1.

71. Allison, *James*, 780. On the idea of new creation, see also Wall, *Community*, 270.

11:13–21.⁷² Either way, the hints alluding to the restoration of creation are clear, evoking the eschatological blessing of superabundant harvest resulting from the removal of the curse of the ground (Gen 3:17–19).⁷³

PRELIMINARY CONCLUSION

Up to this point, we have looked at the church's mission in the letter of James and discovered three main elements. James grants the church two roles essentially limited to the time that precedes the parousia (cf. 5:9) and one that extends beyond it. The first two can be seen as the positive and the negative sides of the church's relationship with society. On the one hand, the church is meant to be a place of blessing and peace. It is called to demonstrate, in the midst of the κόσμος, that obedience to God's law leads to a peaceful and flourishing society. On the other hand, it is a warning to the κόσμος that resisting God's rule will ultimately lead to destruction. Finally, the community serves as a foretaste of the kingdom of God and plays a role in the restoration of creation.

In this picture, two features stand out. God's loving character and his imminent coming as judge both determine the role of the church vis-à-vis the society, and each of these features counters a specific aspect of the κόσμος. By organizing itself according to God's loving character and relieving the suffering of the poor, the church counters the oppressive practices of the κόσμος. By proclaiming God's judgment, the church opposes the attempts of "the world" to live in a closed system apart from God.

The church also lives out another paradox related to time by living in a partial realization of God's kingdom but still awaiting its coming. As an outpost of God's kingdom, the church is *already* organized according to the merciful character of God. It is the place where the poor are respected and cared for, welcomed as brothers and sisters with equal rights and status. Every member of the church is called to shape his or her life according to

---

72. Joel depicts the deliverance and restoration of the land in terms that "suggest the vitality of a new creation" (v. 22). He also mentions the "early and late rain" (v. 23) that first appear in Deut 11:14. See, for instance, Hubbard, *Joel and Amos*, 69–70. McCartney (*James*, 241) sees an allusion to Joel 2:22–23 in Jas 5:7.

73. The idea of abundant harvest and restoration of Eden is common in both Christianity and Judaism. See for instance *1 En.* 10:19; Tgs. Gen 49:12; *Haer.* 5.33.3. For similar ideas in *2 Baruch*, see the comments in Lied, *Other Lands*, 185–241. Since James addresses people "in the diaspora" (1:1), the meaning of "land" must be extended from Palestine (the land promised in Deut 11) to the whole earth, as in many other Second Temple texts (see ref. above).

God's character, manifested in Torah as interpreted by Jesus. The church, therefore, creates a subculture that opposes the practices of the κόσμος by creating a place in which the suffering of the poor is, at least in part, relieved. In the church, as long as its life is organized around love and mercy, the kingdom of God is already, albeit partially, inaugurated. Such a life is possible only through faith, prayer, and receiving the wisdom from above.

At the same time, the church lives entirely in the expectation of the coming of the Lord and hopes for the redemption of creation. Believers live in light of that coming judgment (Jas 2:12–13; 3:1; 4:11–12; 5:9, 12), awaiting in eager anticipation the time when the church will cease to be only an outpost of God's kingdom and enter into the fullness of it. As we saw, the text not only contains multiple allusions to the expectation that God will free the believers from oppression and difficulties (Jas 1:12; 2:12–13; 5:7–8, 10–11), it also gives clear hints that James hopes in the divine intervention to restore creation.

The present role of the church in that eschatological restoration, however, is not yet clear. Is the church called to bring this transformation about? If so, how? If not, what is the church's role? To answer these questions, we now turn to the way the present faithfulness of the Church and the hope of creation are related. We need, therefore, to take a second look at the two passages (Jas 1:17; 5:7–18) that stress the hope of restoration of creation. As we will see, each one emphasizes that the church's faithfulness is instrumental in God's redeeming work, but that this redemption is not brought about by the Church itself.

COMMUNITY HOLINESS AS THE MEANS OF BLESSING THE NATIONS

First-Fruits Metaphor and Abraham's Call to Bless the Nations

There are good reasons to think that the metaphor of first-fruits evokes more than the restoration of creation: it also hints at the responsibility of the community toward the rest of God's creation. The metaphor of first-fruits is by no means a common image for God's people.[74] This begs the question of why James employs it here. A possible explanation is that James chooses that metaphor because it evokes the only OT passage that uses first-fruits as

---

74. Apart from Jas 1:18, it is used for God's people only in Jer 2:3; 2 Thess 2:13; Rev 14:4. Rom 11:16 can also be taken as an indirect reference of God's people as first-fruits.

an image of God's people, Jer 2:3.[75] I propose that such an allusion makes the most sense of Jas 1:18 and its context. Alluding to Jeremiah enables James to tie together the new identity the congregation received, the calling to live a holy life that results from being God's people, and the promise that remaining faithful to God's covenant leads to God fulfilling his promise to restore creation.

First-Fruits Metaphor in Jeremiah

Jeremiah is the only OT author who uses the metaphor of first-fruits to speak of Israel, and comparing God's people to first-fruits is particularly appropriate to his purpose. Jeremiah makes use of a fundamental assumption of his contemporaries—that Israel has a special status before God (i.e., is *holy*)—in order to remind them that their holy status entails specific responsibilities in worship (rejecting idolatry) and in their social organization (caring for the poor), and is tied to the specific purpose of blessing the nations, as God revealed to Abraham (Gen 12:3 is echoed in Jer 4:1–2).

Jeremiah 2:2–3 is the opening oracle of what is sometimes called the "harlotry cycle" (2:1–4:4).[76] This section can be divided in two parts: in the first (2:1–37), Jeremiah exposes Israel's idolatry and rejection of YHWH; in the second (3:1–4:4), Israel is invited to return to God by repenting and transforming its behavior.[77] Hence, the function of these two chapters is to call the people back to repentance, as the climactic oracle in Jer 4:1–4 makes clear.[78] In order to motivate his contemporaries to return to God, Jeremiah contrasts Israel's past experience with its present situation.

Jeremiah stresses the idea—cherished by his contemporaries—that Israel is precious to God because of its special, holy status.[79] The prophet thus hopes to incite his contemporaries to reflect on their misfortune and

75. This has been argued especially by White, *Erstlingsgabe*, 238–60. The reason to hear an echo of Jer 2:3 in Jas 1:18 is laid out in the Appendix.

76. Holladay, *Architecture of Jeremiah 1–20*, 35; DeRoche, "Jeremiah 2:2–3," 364–376.

77. The word "return" (שׁוּב) appears fifteen times in that second section. See Stulman, *Jeremiah*, 47.

78. In Jeremiah, Israel's refusal to repent is the reason God declares his judgment on the nation (in Jer 4:5–6:30).

79. Jeremiah is deeply influenced by the Song of Moses in Deut 32:1–43, a programmatic call of repentance in which Moses speaks about the faithfulness of YHWH, Israel's special status, and how Israel's apostasy would lead to downfall. On the parallel between Jer 2 and Deut 32, see McKane, *Jeremiah*, 29.

to prompt a recognition of their idolatry. Israel is neither a slave nor a servant (Jer 2:14) and therefore need not court any foreign power. This ideal, however, contrasts so obviously with Israel's present condition that it forces the people to reflect on what is happening to them. In that context, Jeremiah suggests that the withdrawal of God's protection is the only explanation: God—who used to hold those who were destroying his people (eating [אָכַל] of his first-fruits, 2:3) accountable—now lets Israel be devoured (אָכַל) by its enemies (3:34). Jeremiah plays on the idea that first-fruits are consecrated to God and cannot be put to common use with impunity (Lev 5:14–16; 22; see also *m. Bik.* 3:10). "Israel is completely devoted to Yahweh, existing for no other reason and available for no other use."[80] Yet by going after idols (Jer 2:11–13, 23, 27–28) and creating alliances with Egypt and Assyria (2:18), Israel defiled itself and so brought all its present trouble upon itself (2:17).

The comment about eating the first-fruits (Jer 2:3)—that is, treating Israel as profane—is most likely addressed to Israel's leaders rather than to foreign nations. The phrase "refers to all those who would put the nation to common use, making it like any other nation, and forgetting the special divine purpose for which Israel was to be set aside. In context, it is not to foreigners that reference is made, but to all those members of the nation who participated in the perversion of national purpose."[81] By treating her own calling lightly, Israel pulled herself away from God's protection and desecrated herself, thereby losing the ability to fulfill God's purpose (4:1–2).

Jeremiah invites Israel to return to God so that God's promise to Abraham (being a blessing to the nations; Gen 12:3 is alluded to in Jer 4:2) will be accomplished.[82] "The restoration of covenant thus will benefit not only Judah but the other nations that derive new life from that covenant."[83] Here, the image of first-fruits in Jeremiah implies that Israel's holiness forms the condition on which the realization of God's promise to bless all nations hangs.

---

80. Brueggemann, *Exile and Homecoming*, 33.

81. Craigie, *Jeremiah 1–25*, 25.

82. Jeremiah 4:1–4 is widely recognized as the concluding oracle of Jer 2:1–4:4, and so responds directly to Jer 2:1–3. Holladay, *Jeremiah*, 62–73; DeRoche, "Jeremiah 2:2–3."

83. Brueggemann, *To Pluck Up*, 46–47.

The Metaphor of First-Fruits in James

We also find this theme in James. Like Jeremiah, James stresses that the honor of being "the first-fruits of God's creation" (1:18) is always accompanied by the call to lead a holy life (1:19–27). Moreover, the mention of "the twelve tribes" in 1:1 is best taken as a reference to the restoration of Israel by means of the reception of the "word of truth" (1:18) or the "implanted word" (1:21). "When James writes to 'the twelve tribes in the diaspora' (1:1) he addresses the Jewish Christian communities as the nucleus of the ongoing messianic renewal of the people of Israel."[84] As such, the community represents those who have received renewed hearts enabling them to live according to God's law (cf. Jer 31[LXX 38]:31–34).[85] We can, therefore, understand the language of birth as the renewal of Israel promised by the prophets.

The main difference between Jeremiah and James resides in the fact that whereas Jeremiah appeals to Israel's ideal (or idealized) past, James thinks of his readers' *present* status. By identifying the people with first-fruits, Jeremiah appeals to the consciousness of the people in order to make them realize that they have betrayed their status. James uses the same image proleptically, as it were, to encourage the community to persevere in the holy way of life that characterizes the renewed people. James's audience has already been restored, and they only need to maintain their calling, not come back to it.

The idea that the consecration of first-fruits implies a greater harvest is not as explicit in James as in Jer 4:1–2, but the temporal dimension of the metaphor highlighted above indicates that this aspect is likely on James's mind as well. Seeing a parallel with Jer 2:3 does not alter the overall meaning of the metaphor; instead it expands and strengthens it. Thus the importance of holy living, as the qualitative dimension of first-fruits, comes to the fore (in keeping with the whole pericope), while preserving its temporal nuance as well (in keeping with the particular phrasing of Jas 1:18).[86] Moreover, hearing Jeremiah's prophecy in Jas 1:18 enables us to

---

84. Bauckham, "James and Jesus," 129. White and Hartin also tie Jas 1:1 and 1:18 as providing a coherent picture of James's understanding of the community as the embodiment of the eschatological restoration of Israel. White, *Erstlingsgabe*, 256–57; Hartin, *Spirituality of Perfection*, 69–70.

85. See Bauckham, *James*, 149; Motyer, *Message of James*, 57; Kamell, "Incarnating," 19–28.

86. Scholars who see the metaphor of first-fruits as having a qualitative value usually fail to acknowledge there is also a temporal idea attached to it. They grant the metaphor

explain the relationship between the qualitative and temporal aspects of the metaphor: as for Jeremiah, maintaining purity is a necessary condition for God to work his salvation through his people.[87]

The Echo of Deuteronomy 11:13–27 in James 5:7–18

The same connection between the holiness of the community and the fulfillment of God's promise also appears in the allusion to Deut 11:13–21 when one pays attention to the meaning and original context of these verses.

Deuteronomy 11:13–21 is located at a key place in Deuteronomy's literary structure: chapters 4–11 (or 5–11) and 12–26 form the two major divisions of the book, the former providing basic stipulations and the latter detailed ones.[88] Hence, Deut 11:13–21 is part of the conclusion to the first section, a chapter that prepares the people to enter the promised land (see especially Deut 11:8–9). On the eve of the conquest, Moses reminds the people of the basic elements of the law they are to keep in order to possess the land. In Deuteronomistic theology, possession of the land depends on obedience (Deut 11:18–25).

Deuteronomy 11:13–21 describes the blessings and the curses on the land in more detail.[89] Here, even the fruitfulness of the land is predicated on Israel's obedience. If Israel obeys God's voice (11:13), God will send the people and the land "the early and the late rain" so that their harvest may

---

only a paraenetic function. See Allison, *James*, 286–87; Konradt, *Christliche Existenz*, 60–66; White, *Erstlingsgabe*, 254–59; Motyer, *Message of James*, 73. The reason may be that when a possible influence of Jeremiah is accepted, Jer 2:3 is read as containing no temporal significance. For instance, Konradt writes, "the designation of Israel in Jer 2:3 is not meant temporally but qualitatively" (*Christliche Existenz*, 61; my translation). This reading of Jeremiah, however, does not take seriously enough Jeremiah's literary unit. Hartin, who takes seriously both the qualitative and the temporal aspect is an exception. Hartin, *Spirituality of Perfection*, 69–74.

87. In Jeremiah, the restoration of creation is not yet in view. Jeremiah speaks of "the nations blessing themselves in him" (likely Israel) and so refers to God's initial promise to Abraham (cf Gen 12:2–3). It is only after the exile that the idea of restoration of creation begins to appear, but it is derived from texts of the Torah, such as Exod 19:5–6, where God is said to rule over the whole earth and where the people is promised to serve as a priestly nation if they abide by God's covenant. It is a common theme in the literature of the Second Temple period.

88. This is von Rad's proposal, refined by George Mendenhall and, subsequently, by Gordon Wenham. See discussion in Thompson, *Deuteronomy*, 18–26.

89. Deuteronomy 11:13–21 is one of the three standard passages (along with Lev 26 and Deut 28–29) describing blessings in response to obedience and curses following covenant disloyalty (cf also Deut 11:26–28).

be plentiful (11:14–15). If, however, the people prove faithless (11:16), rain will not water the land, the earth will not produce its fruit, and the people will perish (11:17). In short, the main theme of Deut 11:13–21 is the relationship between the faithfulness of the people and the fruitfulness of the land.

I propose that James interprets this passage eschatologically and applies it to his communities. We saw earlier that Jas 5:7 and 5:18 are strongly connected to one another by a similar phrase ("the fruit of the earth") and an allusion to Deut 11:13–21, so that they bracket the whole section. Since an *inclusio* usually provides information on the way the section it encloses ought to be read, one can assume that Deut 11:13–21 illuminates the main ideas of Jas 5:7–18. It is likely, then, that James reads Deut 11 eschatologically and as speaking directly to the communities he addresses. In that framework, the imminent conquest of the land becomes the impending entrance into God's kingdom (at the time of the *parousia* of the Lord mentioned in vv. 7 and 8),[90] and taking care of each other sums up Torah obedience.[91] If this proposal is correct, then James is making the same point here as he does in 1:18: the realization of God's eschatological promises are, in some ways, predicated on the holiness of the community. Two other elements support this reading.

First, the OT prophets already gave an eschatological meaning to the promises of Deuteronomy. As we noted earlier, the language of "early and later rain" functions in Joel 2:23, Hos 6:3, and Zech 10:1 as a sign of God's faithfulness and eschatological restoration. James, therefore, simply follows the same logic of interpretation. This is especially likely given that Jas 5:7–18 has a strong eschatological emphasis.[92]

---

90. Passages like Heb 4 and 1 Cor 10:1–6 proves that such interpretations existed early on.

91. Although the command not to grumble against each other (Jas 5:9) also stresses communal wholeness, the emphasis on community is particularly visible in 5:13–18. See especially Albl, "Health Care System," 123–43; Karris, "New Angles." The plural verb in verse 16 stresses further that James is after more than individual healing: "ἰαθῆτε is in the plural, meaning something like, 'so that you all may be healed.' James seems interested in the health of the community, which only comes about as sin is dealt with: ἰαθῆτε hardly speaks of the physical restoration of individual Christians; rather it speaks collectively of the church's health.'" Bowden, "Interpreting Microstructure," 349.

92. Phrases like "the coming of the Lord," (5:7, 8), "the judge is at the door" (5:9), and "the purpose (τέλος) of the Lord" (5:11) convey a clear sense of eschatological hope. The anointing also has an eschatological overtone. See Collins, "James 5:14–16a," 79–91.

Second, the story about the drought brought about by Elijah is by far the best scriptural illustration of Deut 11:13–21, and was traditionally understood as such.[93] In 1 Kgs, the drought on the land results from Ahab's wickedness, and the land is cursed because of Israel's idolatry.[94] Consequently, the end of the drought occurs only after the people repent, reject Baal worship, and return to YHWH. James's allusion to the end of the drought in 1 Kgs 18 has bewildered most interpreters. Many note that Elijah's story contains no explicit mention of prayer and that an example of the power of prayer *for healing* would have been more appropriate to the context of prayer and anointing of the sick of Jas 5:14–15.[95] If, however, one understands the passage as an illustration of the power of prayer for restoration of the community, the allusion to Elijah fits its context remarkably well.[96] Like Elijah, the members of the community are exhorted to seek and pray for the faithfulness of the community. As in Elijah's case, covenant blessings and faithful living are tied together.[97] In light of the eschatological tone of the whole passage and of James's choice to to evoke Gen 1:11 by substituting βλαστάνω for δίδωμι, it seems likely that the covenantal blessing in view is the restoration of the whole creation.

In summary, the language of first-fruits in Jas 1:18 and the *inclusio* of chapter 5 emphasize the same idea: God still works toward the blessings of the nations, as promised to Abraham, and even toward the restoration of creation. Moreover, God's people have an essential role to play in that restorative plan. Surprisingly, however, its main task is not to bring about

93. In Jewish lore, Elijah declares the drought in response to Achab's unbelief that the curses of the covenant have any effect. This is found, among other places, in *y. Sanh.* 10, 28b; *b. Sanh.* 113a. For other references, see Ginzberg, *Legends*, 998. Christian writers also take that story of Elijah as an illustration of the curse of the covenant. In his commentary on Zech 10:1–3 (one of the verses containing the expression "early and late rain"), Didymus the Blind (fourth century) presents a long development on the connection of the drought sent by God and wickedness, and takes the story of Elijah as an illustration. See Didymus the Blind, *Zechariah*, 231–33.

94. See 1 Kgs 18:17–18. Elijah claims that the drought happened "because you [Ahab] have abandoned the commandments of the LORD."

95. For a list of diverging opinion on the way the Elijah illustration fits the context, see Allison, "Liturgical Tradition," 14n41. Allison laconically comments: "commentators flounder here."

96. Karris alludes to this in "New Angles," 215–16. Foster develops the same idea more fully. Foster, *The Significance*, 165–91. See also Kovalishyn, "Elijah," 1027–45.

97. Malachi 4:5–6, in the way it ties the sending of Elijah *in order to avoid the curse on the land*, reflects another association between the figure of Elijah and the curse on the land as a punishment for breaking covenant faithfulness in an eschatological setting.

that restoration but to remain holy—a status members of the community received as a gift when God called them to be *his* people. James gives no indication that the work of the community produces this redemption. On the contrary, the act of restoration will take place at the time of the coming (παρουσία, 5:8) of the Lord. In other words, the eschatological restoration remains God's work and happens at a specific point in time: it is a *crisis* rather than a process.[98] To human eyes, therefore, the *task* of the community (to live faithfully so as to build a community that reflects who God is) and the *result* of its work (the restoration of creation) seem utterly unconnected. According to James, however, they are not.

God-Centered Community

If the community's primary task is to maintain holiness, and if there is little emphasis on transforming society, this immediately raises two questions. Can such a community avoid becoming self-centered? Why does James focus so much on community life at the expense of a missional perspective?

The answer to the first question lies in distinguishing between the task of the community and the task of individuals. James does not ask *the church* to transform society probably because, in its context, it is entirely powerless to do so. He does, however, lay the responsibility on individuals who, because of their social standing, have the means to effect some change. Those who can influence society—in his context, merchants (4:13–17) and landowners (5:1–6)—are commanded to use their wealth to improve the situation of those who are less fortunate—or, at the very least, to not impoverish them even more! Merchants and landowners are exhorted to do the good they are able to do. James expects that faith will have a transformative role in all the ways *individual believers* go about their business, as a result of their growth in maturity.[99] James is not advocating communal

---

98. The coming of the Lord (παρουσία τοῦ κυρίου) is seen as the time of judgment (κρίσις). See Jas 2:13; 5:9, 12.

99. The difference between James's cultural background and ours has to be kept in mind here. A plausible reason for why James does not insist more on the transformation of society is that most of the members of the community could not have any significant influence on society. The situation is radically different in a modern Western context. It seems likely that James would have encouraged Christian politicians and citizens to use all their ability and influence to create a more just society. With more ability or possibility comes more responsibility. Garrett provides a good example of how the message of the merchants can be contextualized for modern Western readers. See Garrett, "Message to the Merchants," 299–315. For a broader attempt of re-contextualization, see also

self-centeredness, but he does not lay the burden of transformation on the group as whole.

As for why James desires the community to focus on holiness more than on mission, four factors can be considered. First, James regards the community as a renewed Israel, and it seems that this perspective informs his understanding of the church's role. James is saturated with the Jewish Scriptures, and he grants the community a similar role to that of Israel in the OT. When the nations witness the wisdom given to Israel through the law (Deut 4:6–8), they are attracted and join Israel in her worship of YHWH.[100] James seems to have in mind the same idea of a movement "from the periphery to the centre" in the case of the church.[101] There are enough indications in the letter to think that James hopes that the quality of life present in the church will attract outsiders. One may surmise, therefore, that he envisions a transformation of society accomplished by having more people forsake the ways of the κόσμος and join the community in response to the way of life it offers.

A second aspect of the answer to this question comes from James's strong opposition to hypocrisy. James does not ask the community to establish the kingdom outside of itself—he wants it to *be* that kingdom. James's view of mission and his passion for integrity cannot be divorced: Christians ought not to attempt to transform society into something they are not themselves able to be. Unless the church *is* the kingdom on earth, it cannot bring it on the earth. God's wisdom has to work its effect in a sphere Christians can influence, and this sphere consists primarily of the Christians themselves and their mutual relationships. James urges teachers to live in accordance with what they preach (3:1), and the same warning may be expanded to the church: the church cannot proclaim what it does not itself experience. Its integrity and holiness are essential to its mission.

Third, James does not entertain great hopes that society will be transformed for the better. As a matter of fact, nothing in the letter points to the idea that society could change so as to move gradually toward an organization that would reflect the kingdom rather than the κόσμος.[102] This

---

Westfall, "Continue," 152–75.

100. See Isa 56:3–8; 66:18–21; Jer 3:17; Mic 4:1–5; Zeph 2:11; 3:9; Zech 8:20–22; 14:16; Mal 1:11.

101. Scobie, "Israel and the Nations," 292. See also Chapter 14 in Wright, *Mission of God*, 454–500.

102. On James's "pessimism" towards society, see Allison, *James*, 609.

pessimistic outlook no doubt derives from the pervasive influence of the κόσμος within every human being.[103] Because the κόσμος is rooted within people (Jas 3:6), society cannot be liberated from the values of the κόσμος unless all men and women have themselves rejected it. Yet people cannot be transformed unless they receive wisdom from above (3:17) and grace (4:5). Human beings are in need of a transformation that occurs only when the word of truth is implanted in them (1:18-25).[104] The idea that one must reject "friendship with the world" presupposes that the choice is made at the individual level, so that the problem of evil is to be fought at a personal level rather than a societal one.

One should not deduce from James's pessimistic view of human nature and society that such a perspective leads to giving up on society. After all, James hopes for society's redemption, not its destruction. Indeed, perhaps pessimism is not the right word at all. For James, remembering that human beings need wisdom from above (3:17) and God's grace (4:5) in order to change is not an excuse to give up, but a reason to persevere. James simply warns his audience not to be surprised if the people around them continue their oppressive behavior and fail to change. Instead, they are to be resolute in face of opposition and continue to live in a way that manifests God's kingdom.

Finally, James insists on the community's holiness because he has great confidence in God's transforming action. The whole letter is filled to the brim with a sense of hope, a hope that is based on the absolute confidence that the future of the individual (1:12; 4:11-12; 5:7-9, 11, 19-20) and of creation (1:18, 5:7-18) lays in God's hand.[105] James sees God—not the church—as the only true agent of transformation in the world. While the setting and context of his audience allows for little hope that they will have any significant influence on society, James reminds them that their obedience possesses a transformational role that far exceeds logical expectations.

---

103. It is also quite probable that James's somber tone comes from the historical context in which members of the community would not have much influence in society. As Westfall notes, "the Jewish Christian population had little power to change policies outside of the confines of the faith community." Westfall, "Continue," 171.

104. On James's negative anthropology (apart from God's help), see Marcus, "Evil Inclination," 606-21; Ellis, *Hermeneutics*, 164-84.

105. Tamez rightly emphasizes the theme of hope in James (*Scandalous Message*, 27-41).

The focus on holy living is not a self-centered attitude but a God-centered one.

SUMMARY AND CONCLUSION

James's understanding of the role of the church is striking in what it excludes and includes. From the evidence we have—and much to the surprise of a modern Christian reader—he seems to have relatively little interest in the proclamation of the gospel. Even more surprisingly, James does not emphasize transformative mission as essential. At the same time, however, he clearly bemoans the state of society. He hopes for its redemption rather than its destruction, and eagerly awaits a time in which the prevalent injustice will be overcome. Nonetheless, James shows no sign of hoping for a gradual transformation of society. Society may be transformed into a less oppressive place through the work of individual believers whose social standing gives them some influence on society, but there is no assurance that it will.

James therefore puts his hope somewhere else and claims that the outcome of faithfulness does not depend on earthly circumstances. According to James, the church overcomes injustice by refusing to take any part in it and by cultivating a holy community, one that truly reflects God's character. The focus on developing a holy community is what binds together every aspect of the church's mission as James sees it.

Developing holiness turns the community into a foretaste of God's kingdom—a community that genuinely cares for the poor and the powerless and so provides an alternative subculture in which human life is valued as it should be. When this happens, the eschatological reversal is partially realized, the future kingdom is locally established, and the life-giving power of God's wisdom is manifested. Developing holiness—which includes valuing the poor—also functions as a prophetic act that warns the κόσμος that its worldview is corrupt in its understanding of human life and value as well as in its view of God. Its view of human life is wrong because wealth and status count for nothing; its view of God is wrong because the eschaton should shape the present life. Finally, the holiness of the community enables God to restore creation. Along with the prophets, James believes that God acts when God's people obey. God's work may not be immediately visible, nor seen as a response to a specific act of obedience, but it is certain all the same. The obedience of the church and God's action in society may happen in completely unrelated areas, and the two may seem to have nothing to do with one another from a human perspective, but James holds that human obedience and prayer have the power to trigger God's act of restoration. To borrow from C. S. Lewis an image that fits the example of Elijah particularly well, "the altar must often be built in one place in order that the fire from heaven may descend somewhere else."[106]

---

106. Lewis, *That Hideous Strength*, 368.

5

Conclusion and Implications

SUMMARY OF ARGUMENT

WE NOTED IN THE introduction to this thesis that the letter of James—and, in fact, a good part of the NT—invites its readers to adopt two stances that seem, at first sight, contradictory. On the one hand, the church is called to differentiate itself from "the world." On the other hand, it is to take an active part in the society in which it lives. Our study has aimed to explain the way James holds to these two poles: important social concerns and strong ethical dualism.

In order to do this, we have proceeded through two main sections. In Chapters 2 and 3, we defined the meaning of "friendship with the world" in James's letter. This enabled us to understand what rejecting that friendship entails. Then, in Chapter 4, we explored the roles James grants to the Christian community with respect to the context in which it lives, both in its relationship with human society and with creation.

In greater detail, we saw in Chapter 2 that the κόσμος represents both a value system and the spiritual power that establishes this system. The κόσμος is also represented as the human matrix on which that system is built, a system where the reality of God—his past and present action, his rule, and his coming judgment—is denied. As a value system, the κόσμος is characterized by two main emphases. First, it values wealth and the status wealth provides more than mercy, and consequently despises the poor. Second, it is marked by a lack of control over one's speech. When people live according to this system of values, they oppose God's rule in an arrogant attempt to place themselves on his throne. We further showed that the problem with "the world" is not merely that such a system exists, but that it has roots within every human being. Through human desires, and particularly through envy, evil powers create dissension, inciting people to fight each other in an attempt to establish their own status. As a consequence, human society becomes the theater of power struggles, reviling speech, oppression, and the like. The fact that the κόσμος has a seat within every human being unless or until it is dethroned by the reception of God's word explains why James offers few signs of hope that human society can be gradually transformed for the better. Those who follow the κόσμος place themselves outside of God's covenant.

In Chapter 3, we established that "friendship with the world" implies adopting this value system and allying oneself with the spiritual powers that promote it. Calls to reject "friendship with the κόσμος" do not speak about sectarian withdrawal coming from contempt for society, nor about disdain for the created order. Rather, refusing to be a "friend of the world" signifies one's readiness to hate evil, especially in the forms in which it has become socially acceptable. In James's context, contempt for the poor and reviling speech are the main elements of socially acceptable forms of evil. The metaphor of friendship also enables James to develop the theme of double-mindedness in the letter. By choosing that image, he forces his readers to think about their ultimate allegiance and to choose between the κόσμος and God. Failing to make a choice results in double-mindedness. "Friendship with the world" *must* be rejected in order to be available to develop "friendship with God," a life-long walk of single-minded obedience, implying steadfastness in trials and leading to the development of spiritual maturity. Not doing so means stepping outside of covenant—which eventually, leads to death.

Also in Chapter 3, we saw that the metaphor of friendship concerned the individual rather than the community. Though James maintains a strong communal concern throughout his letter, here he stresses the choice that every individual member of the community must make regarding his or her fundamental allegiance. By asking his readers to take a stance on this issue, James confronts everyone with his or her own responsibility to submit to God's commands and let the "word of truth" take deep root within him or her. By so doing, James redefines the people of God as the community of all those who receive wisdom from above and who, like Abraham, walk in this wisdom. In other words, the people of God is composed of individuals

CONCLUSION AND IMPLICATIONS

who let the word of truth uproot evil desires from their hearts and develop God-like characters. By actively rejecting the κόσμος and its deceitful values, the community learns to love others according to God's royal law.

In Chapter 4, we unpacked the task James lays upon the church, and discovered that his motivation is thoroughly eschatological. In keeping with his description of the problem of evil—sin is rooted in human desires rather than in social systems—James aims not at reforming society but at creating counter-cultural communities free from the values of the κόσμος. Such freedom is gained by practicing the "law of freedom." Putting God's command into practice reshapes the values of the community so that it becomes a place where wealth and status are unimportant. Such communities become outposts of God's kingdom, living in tune with the "royal law." They become, that is, places where the true king—the one who authored the law, who will judge everyone, and whose universal reign is about to begin—already reigns. As such, the behavior of these communities embodies God's character and interaction with humanity by showing mercy and care for those who are crushed but opposition against those who oppress others. It is the character of the God they worship—an extravagantly generous and merciful God—that provides the ground and pattern for all of James's social imperatives. The practice of supporting and honoring the poor thus stems not from a pragmatic desire to make society a better place, but from a commitment to practice the law of freedom. Even blessing society in the present time is eschatologically motivated.

Honoring the poor and seeking peace are simply the concrete expressions of the "wisdom from above," the way of life the Creator always meant for his creatures. To borrow an image from Tolkien, those who live according to the wisdom of above are those whose song remains tuned to the harmony of the Great Music.[1] Those who adopt the values of the κόσμος, on the other hand, create dissonances in that harmony. For them, the existence of a group that preserves the original theme of the melody sounds a warning that they will not keep their position in the orchestra if they persist in playing their own tune, thereby disregarding their fellow singers and the conductor.

Finally, we also demonstrated that James grants the community a crucial role in the restoration of creation. Surprising as this may sound, James implies that the restoration of the created order is predicated on the purity and wholeness of the congregation. This is not to suggest that the church produces that restoration—God is the one who brings it about.

---

1. Tolkien, *Silmarillion*, 1–5.

Nonetheless, James invites his readers to open themselves to the idea that the simple acts of creating a peaceful community that cares for the sick among them has a spiritual outcome that far surpasses the logical consequence of these actions. When the community cares for its sick members, God heals his ailing creation.

We are now in a position to answer our initial question: James can hold social concerns (care for the poor) and cultural differentiation (rejecting friendship with the world) together because these things are two sides of the same coin. The κόσμος represents the perverted worldview and the spiritual powers that lend it its power, a worldview that leads to oppression. Rejecting it is the only way to properly relate to creatures and creation—to live the way God always intended for humanity. Refusing to be a friend of the world has nothing to do with misanthropy, nor with any kind of escapist spirituality. Instead, it is the complete rejection of all the ways in which evil defiles and destroys God's creation.

IMPLICATIONS

The research presented above leads to a number of implications regarding a biblical theology of culture. The following discussion derives uniquely from James's epistle, and a comprehensive biblical theology must be balanced and completed with the teaching of other books of Scripture. The five points below stand out as the most striking elements in James's contribution regarding the relationship of the church and society.

The first two points flow from the idea that the κόσμος has a seat in every human being. First, the fact that the κόσμος resides in human beings makes it clear that the problem of evil is not primarily a systemic issue, but a personal one. It follows, therefore, that one does not do justice to James's thought when one takes him primarily as a social activist or reformer. James insists on love and care for the poor and the marginalized—probably more so than any other biblical author—but his aim is not primarily to transform society. He is first of all concerned that the church's life be a faithful representation of God's character. This does not imply that James does not care about the transformation of society. Instead, he believes that true transformation happens only when people are themselves transformed by the implanted word.

Our second point derives directly from the first: for James, the church's role is prophetic rather than transformational. In other words, its role is to bear witness to God, to demonstrate his wisdom and reflect his heart by seeking peace and living in harmony, and to remind oppressors that their domination will soon come to an end. Justice will ultimately triumph. To be sure, the church also has a transformational role to play, but this comes as a result of its prophetic ministry. Transforming the organization of society without also restoring the hearts of those who take part in that society does not bring any lasting change.

Third, James reminds us that hating evil and loving God belong together. This is where one can—and should—place James's critique of society. While James does not aim at reforming society directly, he has a keen sense of the ways injustice takes root in society, and he does not want the church to take any part in it. He wants the Christian community to take a firm stance against any kind of behavior that negates the equal dignity of the poor. This, I believe, is one of the greatest challenges currently facing the Western church. In an age of alarmingly large—and still growing—gaps between rich and poor, James's letter calls believers to refuse to participate in the world's iniquitous system. Although these issues are extremely complex, the difficulty of taking a firm stance is, sadly, more often the result of unwillingness to let go of the advantages offered by this unjust system, not a lack of clarity about what could be done.

By stressing hatred of evil, James reminds us that one cannot affirm everything. On the one hand, James insists that obedient faith leads to a life that overflows with mercy and generosity. This stands out in even a cursory reading of the letter, and while living up to this standard is no trivial invitation, the message itself is accepted by most. The call to love one's neighbor possesses an undeniable appeal and is rarely despised. James also insists, however, that love of one's neighbor must go hand in hand with hatred of evil. Either evil is utterly rejected and uprooted, or love will eventually be stifled. True love is selective: some things have to be hated precisely because they ultimately render love for one's neighbor impossible. That which opposes the royal law must be set aside, no matter how deeply anchored in culture. This is also a stern reminder for a church that is often tempted to replace love with tolerance.

Fourth, James's view of the mission of the Church is eschatologically motivated. Although he does not spell out the reasons for this—he simply assumes the imminent coming of the Lord—we can posit that his view has at least two benefits. One is that grounding his ethics in an eschatological outlook enables him to perceive the failure of his own society more clearly.[2]

---

2. Since the church is primarily called to live faithfully according to God's law,

To put it differently, James's ethic is less contingent on the way society is organized in the present because it is grounded in a reality yet to be revealed. The other benefit is that the eschatological outlook enables him to offer powerful encouragement to those who live in difficult circumstances, especially those who suffer because of their commitment to faithfulness. We suspect that the desire to transform society would not be a sufficient motivation to heed James's command to reject the κόσμος when the personal cost is high. After all, the hope of creating a better society can function as a motivating factor only when one has good reason to believe that persevering through hardship will eventually bring about the desired transformation. When no amelioration is expected in the foreseeable future—which was no doubt the case for some of James's original readers, and is still the case for many Christians today—the call to mission must be rooted in something deeper than the belief that one's work will produce a better society.

The fifth implication follows from this: the success or failure of mission does not depend upon the church's activity, but upon its faithfulness.[3] In James, the mission of the Church is not goal-oriented but God-oriented. By striving toward maturity and practising the word, the church's mission is carried forward. In James's terminology, the harvest results from fleshing out the wisdom from above in one's everyday life. In a sense, one may even say that speaking of a "mission of the church" does not do justice to James's thought. The church has a purpose and an important role to play in God's larger plan of redemption, but it is God—not the church—who brings it about. The only real role of God's people, according to James, is to be faithful to the covenant. When this condition is met, the fruit of obedience far transcends its logical outcome. As we saw, the fate of the church and of the world are tied together, so that the church's faithfulness possesses cosmic repercussions. In this view, James stands in perfect continuity with OT theology and the connection drawn between election and blessing of the nations in Jer 2:1–4:4 (especially 4:1–2) and elsewhere.[4] This perspective is indeed one of hope.

---

ethics is an integral part of mission for James.

3. One should note here that faithfulness is defined by James in practical terms, as an activity or concrete behavior.

4. Commenting on this passage, Wright writes: "Let Israel return to their mission (to be the people of YHWH, worshiping him exclusively and living according to his moral demands), and God can return to his mission—blessing the nations." Wright, *Mission of God*, 241. As we have seen, James shares that perspective.

Appendix

METHODOLOGICAL TOOLS TO ASSESS OT ALLUSIONS

IN THIS THESIS, I have proposed that the community is instrumental to the restoration of creation, an argument I grounded in two allusions to OT passages: Jer 2:3 in Jas 1:18, and Deut 11:13–21 in Jas 5:7–20. The idea that these passages in James do not point to a single verse but rather to the OT context of these verses makes it necessary to demonstrate that there is solid evidence for this. This is the goal of this appendix.

In order to establish with reasonable likelihood that James borrows from these texts, I will follow Richard Hays's criteria for validating OT allusions.[1] These seven criteria are:[2]

1. *Availability.* The source text . . . must be available to the writer . . .[3]

2. *Volume.* There is a significant degree of verbatim repetition of words or syntactical patterns.[4]

3. *Recurrence.* There are references in the immediate context (or elsewhere by the same author) to the same OT context from which the purported allusion derives.[5]

---

1. Hays, Echoes, 29–32.

2. The summary offered here is an abbreviated version of Beale, Handbook, 33.

3. This criterion is met by default when it comes to Scripture. It is more useful when it comes to allusions to apocryphal texts or sayings of Jesus.

4. Hays notes that other factors, such as the distinctiveness and prominence of an OT passage, also influence the *volume* of an allusion. Hays, Echoes, 30.

5. Although I will keep this criterion for the sake of completeness, its value is greatly

APPENDIX

4. *Thematic Coherence*. The alleged OT allusion is suitable and satisfying in that its meaning in the OT not only thematically fits into the NT writer's argument but also illuminates it . . .

5. *Historical Plausibility*. There is plausibility that the NT writer could have intended such an allusion and that the audience could have understood the NT writer's use of it . . .[6]

6. *History of Interpretation* . . . others have observed the allusion . . .[7]

7. *Satisfaction*. With or without confirmation from the preceding six criteria, does the proposed allusion and its interpretative usage make sense in the immediate context? Does it illuminate the surrounding context?

DEUTERONOMY 11:13–21 IN JAMES 5:7–20

As we saw, Jas 5:7 and 5:18 are linked by a double mention of the "fruit of the earth" (5:7: τὸν τίμιον καρπὸν τῆς γῆς; 5:18: τὸν καρπὸν αὐτῆς [i.e., τῆς γῆς]), and each of these verses borrows a phrase from a different verse from Deut 11:13–21, the second section of the *Shema*.

The observations made above imply that we don't have to discuss the criteria of *availability* and of *historical plausibility*; they are met by default. Moreover, since James quotes the *Shema* in 2:19, alludes to it in 4:12, and may also do so in 1:12 and 2:5, the criterion of *recurrence* is also fulfilled.[8] Finally, given the importance of the text at the time, the *volume* of the allusion will be high even if the number of words repeated verbatim is few.

The expression "the early and the late [rain]" (πρόϊμος καὶ ὄψιμος) in Jas 5:7 echoes a phrase (πρόϊμος καὶ ὄψιμος ὑετός) that appears for the first time in Deut 11:14 and is found four other times in prophetic literature (in Jer 5:24; Hos 6:3; Joel 2:23; Zech 10:1).[9] Various attempts have been made

---

diminished for a short book like James. Hays penned these criteria when dealing with the entire Pauline corpus.

6. This criterion is mainly designed to protect against anachronistic projection in the mind of the author. In other words, the point is to make sure the proposed allusion has its place in the Jewish universe of the first century.

7. Both Hays and Beale see this as the least determinative criterion. Hays, Echoes, 31; Beale, Handbook, 33.

8. Edgar, "Love-Command," 9–22.

9. Deuteronomy 11:14 reads: "he will give rain for your land according to its time, the early and the late rain" (καὶ δώσει τὸν ὑετὸν τῇ γῇ σου καθ᾽ ὥραν πρόϊμον καὶ ὄψιμον). James omits the word "rain," and some MSS add either "rain" (ὑετός: A, P, Ψ, . . .) or

to explain James's language here, either taking the expression to be a "proverbial expression"[10] or as evidence for a Palestinian setting of the epistle,[11] but it is impossible to ground these proposals in any actual data. A search in the *Thesaurus Linguae Graecae* reveals that the expression does not exist outside of biblical and patristic literature.[12] Apart from two references, the Church Fathers use the phrase only when they quote one of these five verses. We can, therefore, be almost certain that the phrase derives from the LXX. Moreover, given that the words πρόϊμος καὶ ὄψιμος represent an unusual phrase, they are sufficiently distinctive to assume they would be heard as a reference to another text. Finally, we can note that it is quite possible that the prophets themselves borrowed the phrase "early and late rain" from Deuteronomy. Apart from Hos 6:3, the three other texts show remarkable thematic similarity to Deut 11:13–21.[13]

In Jas 5:18, the phrase "and the earth gave its fruit" (ἡ γῆ ἐβλάστησεν τὸν καρπὸν αὐτῆς, 5:18) is almost the exact reversal of the curse found in Deut 11:17.

| Deut 11:17 | ἡ | γῆ | | οὐ | δώσει | τὸν καρπὸν αὐτῆς |
| James 5:18 | ἡ | γῆ | | | ἐβλάστησεν | τὸν καρπὸν αὐτῆς |

Only two other verses would come that close to the wording of James.

| Psa 84:13 | ἡ | γῆ | ἡμῶν | οὐ | δώσει | τὸν καρπὸν αὐτῆς |
| Psa 66:7 | | γῆ | | | ἔδωκεν | τὸν καρπὸν αὐτῆς[14] |

"fruit" (καρπός: ℵ, ...). Only the former expression is attested in the LXX.

10. Dibelius, *James*, 244. Laws thinks that the expression was well known because it was used in the Shema, but believes it had come to be used independently from its original context. Although possible, we do not have the slightest evidence to support this proposal. Laws, *James*, 212.

11. Davids, *The Epistle of James*, 183–84. Scot McKnight (*Letter of James*, 409n184) agrees tentatively.

12. If one removes texts written by the church fathers or after the tenth century (i.e., texts that have been influenced by the LXX), only one author comes close to what we find in James. Eudoxus of Cnidus (fourth century BCE) writes about "τῶν καρπῶν οἱ πρώιμοι καὶ οἱ ὄψιμοι εὐφορήσουσιν." in *Atrom*. F. Boll, *Codices Germanici, Catalogus Codicum Astrologorum Graecorum 7* (Brussels: Lamertin, 1908), 183–87, http://stephanus.tlg.uci.edu.ezproxy.library.ubc.ca/Iris/Cite?1358:002:9334.

13. More on that below.

14. Although this may be a detail, neither of these verses specifies that the rain comes "from heaven," unlike Jas 5:18 and Deut 11:17 (implicitly in Deut 11:17, explicitly in

In summary, in each case (Jas 5:7 and 5:18) the extent of verbatim agreement between the two texts is too short to be considered a quotation, but sufficient to be distinctive and recognizable. The *volume* criteria is thus met for each allusion. It is in principle possible, but less likely, that each of these phrases could be derived from other verses. For one thing, these other verses were less well known as the *Shema* (less *volume*) and lack support from other passages in James (lack of *recurrence*). Moreover, these echoes, appearing in two verses connected by similar wording, strengthen each other by their proximity. If either were to be taken on their own, we would be less certain that Deut 11 lays in the background—but since we have two close allusions to the same OT paragraph, their mutual case is strengthened by a "cluster effect."[15] Finally, Deut 11:13–21 is the first occurrence of each of these phrases in Scripture. We can, therefore, conclude that the intrinsic evidence for the allusion is quite strong.

The *thematic coherence* between the two passages and the fact that intertextuality provides a satisfactory reading (*satisfaction* criterion) has been discussed elsewhere in this thesis. In sum, apart for the *history of interpretation* criterion, Hays's criteria are met.[16]

JEREMIAH 2:3 IN JAMES 1:18

I have shown in the body of this thesis that these two passages have close *thematic connections* and that hearing an echo of Jer 2:3 in Jas 1:18 leads to a *satisfactory* reading. In addition, the criteria of *availability* and *historical plausibility* are clearly met, simply because the text in question is drawn from the Jewish Scriptures. In this appendix, therefore, I will discuss the criterion of *history of interpretation* and provide a few more arguments that increase the *thematic coherence* between the two passages, show a significant amount of *recurrence*, and raise the *volume* of the allusion.

Here again, the history of interpretation of Jas 1:18 does not bring much support to our reading. If nearly every commentator cites Jer 2:3 as a parallel to Jas 1:18, they rarely go beyond a simple mention of another

---

Deut 11:11).

15. The expression "cluster effect" is borrowed from Johnson, who makes a similar argument for the use of Lev 19:12–19 in James. Johnson, "Leviticus 19," 394.

16. As noted above, I am not aware of anyone defending these two allusions, so the criteria of *history of interpretation* is not met. Hays himself, however, recognizes that "this criterion should rarely be used as a negative test to exclude proposed echoes that commend themselves on other grounds." Hays, *Echoes*, 31.

referent where the image of first-fruits is applied to God's people. They understand the parallel to be merely linguistic, without any bearing on the interpretation of James. To my knowledge, only Joel White proposes that James follows Jeremiah closely.[17] The fact Jeremiah is not granted the right to shed light on James might say more, however, about the hermeneutics of NT readers than about James's intentions.

We have shown in the thesis that the themes of the relevant passages in James and Jeremiah are identical. Both stress the idea that being God's first-fruits is always accompanied by the call to lead a holy life, and both argue that the holiness of God's people is a crucial element to the accomplishment of their calling. In addition to these major thematic parallels, a number of minor connections between the two texts are also noteworthy. Both stress the faithfulness of God's character (Jas 1:17; cf. Jer 2:5, 31), warn against forgetting the law (Jas 1:24–25; cf. Jer 2:32; 3:21), insist on mercy towards the poor (Jas 1:27; cf. Jer 2:34), and speak of the uselessness of a superficial worship accompanied by evil deeds (Jas 1:26–27; cf. Jer 3:5). None of these elements carry much weight on their own, but it is striking that so many ties exist between the two passages. This points to great *thematic coherence* between the two passages.

When it comes to the *volume* of the citation, the situation seems, at first, hopeless. The echo of Jer 2:3 in Jas 1:18 is of a different nature than those echoes discussed above. Whereas Jas 5:7 and 5:18 share some phrases from Deut 11, no such connection exists between Jer 2:3 and Jas 1:18. While both authors speak of "first-fruits," James speaks of ἀπαρχή where the LXX uses ἀρχή (translating the Hebrew רֵאשִׁית). The texts are thus related not by shared words, but only by a similar concept. In terms of Hays's criteria, the *volume* is low. However, the vocabulary used to describe first-fruits is somewhat fluid in both Greek and Hebrew.[18] Moreover, as White notices, the fact that Jer 2:3 is the only passage from which James could derive his image actually strengthens the possibility that he refers to that text.[19] In

---

17. See White, Erstlingsgabe, 238–60. Allison cites W. Dodd (1770) as defending an allusion to Jer 2:3 as well. Allison, James, 283n189.

18. The terms used are ἀπαρχή, ἀρχή, ἅγιος, and πρωτογένημα in the LXX; רֵא, תְּרוּמָה בִּכּוּרִים, שִׂית in the MT. See Silva, "ἀπαρχή κτλ.," 1:102–15.

19. White, Erstlingsgabe, 238–60. White devotes an entire study to the theme of first-fruits in the NT and takes the absence of other possible referents as an important criterion to decide whether or not a NT passage alludes to an OT one. He proposes four criteria to decide whether an echo is probable or not, and concludes that all four criteria are fulfilled in the case of Jas 1:18. His criteria are the following: (1) level of concordance

APPENDIX

other words, the specificity of the image—and the existence of more common metaphors that could have fulfilled a similar function—significantly raises the volume of the allusion. Authors who want to insist on Israel's special status usually employ other images, referring to Israel as God's firstborn son (or simply "son"),[20] God's inheritance (or "chosen part"),[21] or simply as a holy people.[22] The image coined by Jeremiah is unique in the Jewish Scriptures. Finally, the fact that Jer 2:3 was part of the early Jewish liturgy implies that the text was already well known in the first century.[23]

Finally, the criterion of *recurrence* is met because James refers several times to Jeremiah, especially in Jas 1. As we have seen, Jas 1:18 has to be read together with Jas 1:1, each verse illuminating the other and forming a clear picture of James's understanding of his audience as restored Israel.[24] This implies that Jas 1:18–21 is probably a meditation on the promise that God's law will be written on the heart of the restored people (Jer 31[LXX 38]:31–34).[25] This connection with Jeremiah is made all the more likely by the fact that, "within the final form of the book of Jeremiah, these two passages [Jer 2:2–4:2 and Jer 30–31] stand in an important connection to one another, somewhat as mirror opposites."[26] Another reference to Jeremiah occurs in James's comment about boasting in 1:9–10, which is

---

in the ways terminology is used in each texts ("Übereinstimmungsgrad"); (2) lack of cross-connections with other texts ("Querverbindungen"); (3) overall coherence of the later text if the earlier text is assumed; (4) explicative potential of the earlier text. Criteria 1, 3, and 4 overlap with Hays's criteria. White's second criterion, however, is particular to him, and it makes a great deal of sense.

20. See Exod 4:22; Jer 31:9; Jub. 2:20; 19:29; 3 En. 44:10; 4 Ezra 6:58; LAB 18:6; 32:16. For Israel described as God's son, see Deut 14:1; 32:6; Jer 31:20; Hos 11:1.

21. See Deut 9:26; 32:9; Jer 12:10; Zech 2:6–12, Esth; 13:15–16; Sir 17:17–18; 2 Macc 1:25; 2 Macc 14:15; 3 Macc 6:3; Ps. Sol. 14:5. In Christian writers, see 1 Clem 29:2; Barn 14:4.

22. Deut 7:6; 14:2, 21; 26:18–19; 28:9; Is 30:19; 62:12; Hos 12:1; Dan 7:27; 12:7; 2 Macc 15:24; 3 Macc 2:6.

23. The time at which prophetic readings was standardized is debated, but the most likely guess is that it originated sometime during the first century. See Fishbane, Haftarot, xx–xxi.

24. Bauckham, "James and Jesus," 129; Hartin, Spirituality of Perfection, 69–70.

25. Bauckham, James, 149; Motyer, Message of James, 57; Kamell, "Incarnating," 19–28.

26. Burnett, "Changing Gods," 289. As important parallels, one can note the following: God protecting Israel in Jer 30:20 echoes Jer 2:3; Israel will be a virgin again (Jer 31:4, 21) and not be a prostitute (Jer 2:20; 3:1, 6, 9) anymore; Jer 30:8 uses the exact same language as Jer 2:20; Jer 30–31, like Jer 3:6–13, is concerned with the northern kingdom and Judah.

almost certainly influenced by Jer 9:22–23.[27] There are thus at least three allusions to Jeremiah in the first chapter of James's letter.[28] In addition, it is generally recognized that James's condemnation of the rich in 5:5 borrows its language from Jer 12:3.[29]

Again, we find that all the validating criteria proposed by Hays are met. The reading proposed in this thesis corresponds overall with the reading done by scholars such as Joel White, Richard Bauckham, and Matthias Konradt. However, these scholars overlook the fact that Jeremiah's image includes a missional dimension to election of God's people. This emphasis is lost because the message of Jeremiah is taken in isolation (or, at best, studied in its immediate context) and because the entire literary unit is not considered. When we take the entire section (Jer 2:2–4:2) into account, it becomes clear that the image of first-fruits includes a missional element tied to the holiness of God's people.[30] The argument that this element also plays a central place in James's letter is one of the original contributions of this thesis.

---

27. Williams, "Of Rags and Riches," 273–82.

28. Jeremiah's temple sermon (7:1–15) and his call to look after the orphans and widows (Jer 7:6) may have been an inspiration to Jas 1:27, but the theme is so pervasive in the OT that James's call most likely has no specific referent.

29. See Allison, James, 683. In Jas 2:7, the expression "the name which was called upon you" (τὸ καλὸν ὄνομα τὸ ἐπικληθὲν ἐφ' ὑμᾶς) is derived from OT language. Here again, a possible referent—cited in NA28—is Jer 14:9, but other verses could work just as well (see 2 Chr 7:14; Baruch 2:15; Dan 9:19).

30. Two reading from Jeremiah 1–4 (Jer 1:1–2:3; 2:4–28 + 4:1–2) are read as haftarot, and they are often read together. The fact that the second reading is concluded by Jer 4:1–2 likely indicates that these verse were already understood to be the conclusion of the whole section early on. See Fishbane, Haftarot, 262–69.

Bibliography

Adam, A. K. M. *James: A Handbook on the Greek Text.* BHGNT. Waco, TX: Baylor University Press, 2013.
Adamson, James B. *The Epistle of James.* NICNT. Grand Rapids: Eerdmans, 1976.
———. *James: The Man and His Message.* Grand Rapids: Eerdmans, 1989.
Albl, Martin C. "'Are Any among You Sick?': The Health Care System in the Letter of James." *JBL* 121 (2002) 123–43.
Aletti, Jean-Noël. "James 2,14–26: The Arrangement and Its Meaning." *Biblica* 95 (2014) 88–101.
Allison, Dale C. *A Critical and Exegetical Commentary on the Epistle of James.* ICC. New York: Bloomsbury, 2013.
———. "Eldad and Modad." *JSP* 21 (2011) 99–131.
———. "The Fiction of James and Its Sitz Im Leben." *RB* 108 (2001) 529–570.
———. "A Liturgical Tradition behind the Ending of James." *JSNT* 34 (2011) 3–18.
Alonso Schökel, Luis. "James 5:2 [sic] and 4:6." *Biblica* 54 (1973) 73–76.
Amphoux, Christian-Bernard. "Une relecture du chapitre I de l'Épître de Jacques." *Biblica* 59 (1978) 554–61.
Assaël, Jacqueline, and Elian Cuvillier. "À propos de la traduction et de l'interprétation de Jacques 2.1." *NTS* 57 (2011) 145–51.
———. *Epître de Saint-Jacques.* Geneva: Labor et Fides, 2013.
Baker, William R. *Personal Speech-Ethics in the Epistle of James.* Tübingen: Mohr Siebeck, 1995.
———. "The Community of Believers in James." In *New Testament Church: The Challenge of Developing Ecclesiologies*, edited by John Harrison and James D. Dvorak, 208–25. McMaster Biblical Studies Series. Eugene, OR: Pickwick, 2012.
Baltzly, Dirk, and Nick Eliopoulos. "The Classical Ideals of Friendship." In *Friendship: A History*, edited by Barbara Caine, 1–64. 2009. Reprint, London: Routledge, 2014.
Barclay, John M. G. "Chapter 4: Jews in a Diaspora Environment: Some Analytical Tools." In *Jews in the Mediterranean Diaspora: From Alexander to Trajan (323 BCE–117 CE)*, 82–102. Edinburgh: T&T Clark, 1996.
Barton, John. "Imitation of God in the Old Testament." In *The God of Israel*, edited by Robert P. Gordon, 35–46. Cambridge: Cambridge University Press, 2007.
Batten, Alicia J. "The Degraded Poor and the Greedy Rich: Exploring the Language of Poverty and Wealth in James." In *Social Sciences and Biblical Translation*, edited by Dietmar Neufeld, 65–77. Atlanta: SBL, 2008.

BIBLIOGRAPHY

———. *Friendship and Benefaction in James*. 2010. Reprint, Emory Studies in Early Christianity 15. Atlanta: SBL, 2017.

———. "God in the Letter of James: Patron or Benefactor?" *NTS* 50 (2004) 257–72.

———. "Unworldly Friendship, the Epistle of Straw Reconsidered." Thesis, University of St. Michael's College, 2000. Accessed November 20, 2017. https://tspace.library.utoronto.ca/handle/1807/10519.

Bauckham, Richard. "James, 1 and 2 Peter, Jude." In *It Is Written: Scripture Citing Scripture: Essays in Honour of Barnabas Lindars, SSF*, edited by D. A. Carson and H. G. M. Williamson, 303–17. Cambridge: Cambridge University Press, 1988.

———. "James, 1 Peter, Jude and 2 Peter." In *Vision for the Church: Studies in Early Christian Ecclesiology*, edited by Markus Bockmuehl and Michael B. Thompson, 153–66. Edinburgh: A&C Black, 1997.

———. "James and Jesus." In *The Brother of Jesus: James the Just and His Mission*, edited by Bruce Chilton and Jacob Neusner, 100–37. Louisville: Westminster John Knox, 2001.

———. *James: Wisdom of James, Disciple of Jesus the Sage*. NTR. London: Routledge, 1999.

———. "The Relevance of Extra-Canonical Jewish Texts to New Testament Study." In *Hearing the New Testament: Strategies for Interpretation*, edited by Joel B. Green, 90–108. Grand Rapids: Eerdmans, 1995.

———. "The Spirit of God in Us Loathes Envy: James 4:5." In *Holy Spirit and Christian Origins: Essays in Honor of James D G Dunn*, edited by Graham M. Stanton et al., 270–81. Grand Rapids: Eerdmans, 2004.

———. "The Tongue Set on Fire by Hell [James 3.6]." In *The Fate of the Dead : Studies on the Jewish and Christian Apocalypses*, 93:119–31. NovTSup. Leiden: Brill, 1998.

Beale, G. K. *Handbook on the New Testament Use of the Old Testament: Exegesis and Interpretation*. Grand Rapids: Baker Academic, 2012.

———. *We Become What We Worship: A Biblical Theology of Idolatry*. Downers Grove, IL: InterVarsity, 2008.

Bede. *The Commentary on the Seven Catholic Epistles of Bede the Venerable*. Translated by David Hurst. Cistercian Studies Series 82. Kalamazoo, MI: Cistercian Publications, 1985.

Bertram, Georg. "Εὐεργετέω, Εὐεργέτης, Εὐεργεσία." In *TDNT* 2:654–655. Edited by Gerhard Kittel and Gerhard Friedrich. Translated by Geoffrey William Bromiley. Grand Rapids: Eerdmans, 1985.

———. "Ὁρμή, Ὅρμημα, Ὁρμάω, Ἀφορμή." In *TDNT* 5:467–472. Edited by Gerhard Kittel and Gerhard Friedrich. Translated by Geoffrey William Bromiley. Grand Rapids: Eerdmans, 1985.

Black, Matthew. "Critical and Exegetical Notes on Three New Testament Texts: Hebrews 6:11, Jude 5, James 1:27." In *Apophoreta: Festschrift Für Ernst Haenchen Zu Seinem Siebzigsten Geburtstag*, edited by Walther Eltester, 39–45. BZNW. Berlin: Alfred Töpelmann, 1964.

Blomberg, Craig L., and Mariam Kamell. *James*. ZECNT. Grand Rapids: Zondervan, 2008.

Borg, Marcus J. *Meeting Jesus Again for the First Time: The Historical Jesus and the Heart of Contemporary Faith*. San Francisco: HarperCollins, 1994.

Bowden, Andrew M. "Interpreting Microstructure through Discourse Analysis, with Specific Application to the Text of James 5:13–18." ThM thesis, Southeastern Baptist

Theological Seminary, 2011. Accessed January 31, 2018. https://search.proquest.com/religion/docview/921979351/abstract/CF783B19B1A34760PQ/3.

Bratcher, Robert Galveston. "The Meaning of Kosmos, 'World', in the New Testament." *BT* 31 (1980) 430–34.

Brosend, William F. *James and Jude*. NCBC. Cambridge: Cambridge University Press, 2004.

Brueggemann, Walter. *A Commentary on Jeremiah: Exile and Homecoming*. Grand Rapids: Eerdmans, 1998.

———. *To Pluck Up, to Tear Down: A Commentary on the Book of Jeremiah 1–25*. Grand Rapids: Eerdmans, 1988.

Burnett, Joel S. "Changing Gods: An Exposition of Jeremiah 2." *RevExp* 101 (2004) 289–300.

Calvin, Jean. *Commentaries on the Catholic Epistles*. Edinburgh: Calvin Translation Society, 1855.

Cambe, Michel. "Isidore de Péluse, interprète de Jacques 3,6: 'le cosmos de l'injustice', 'la roue de l'existence.'" *RHPR* 92 (2012) 387–411.

Cantinat, Jean. *Les Épîtres de Saint Jacques et de Saint Jude*. Paris: Gabalda, 1973.

Chaine, Joseph. *L'Épitre de Saint Jacques*. Paris: Gabalda, 1927.

Chester, Andrew, and Ralph P. Martin. *The Theology of the Letters of James, Peter, and Jude*. NTT. Cambridge: Cambridge University Press, 1994.

Cheung, Luke L. *The Genre, Composition, and Hermeneutics of the Epistle of James*. 2nd ed. Eugene, OR: Wipf & Stock, 2006.

Cicero. *On the Good Life*. Translated by Michael Grant. London: Penguin, 2005.

Collins, John C. "James 5:14–16a: What Is the Anointing For?" *Presbyterion* 23 (1997) 79–91.

Corley, Jeremy. "Friendship According to Ben Sira." In *Der Einzelne Und Seine Gemeinschaft Bei Ben Sira*, edited by Renate Egger-Wenzel and Ingrid Krammer, 65–72. BZAW 270. Berlin: Walter de Gruyter, 1998.

Craigie, Peter C. *Jeremiah 1–25*. WBC 26. Grand Rapids: Zondervan, 1991.

D'Angelo, Mary Rose. "Abba and 'Father': Imperial Theology and the Jesus Traditions." *JBL* 111 (1992) 611–30.

Danker, Frederick W. "Bridging St. Paul and the Apostolic Fathers: A Study in Reciprocity." *Currents in Theology and Mission* 15 (1988) 84–94.

Davids, Peter H. "Controlling the Tongue and the Wallet: Discipleship in James." In *Patterns of Discipleship in the New Testament*, edited by Richard N. Longenecker, 225–47. Grand Rapids: Eerdmans, 1996.

———. *The Epistle of James: A Commentary on the Greek Text*. 1982. Reprint, NIGTC. Grand Rapids: Eerdmans, 2013.

———. *James*. NIBC 15. Peabody, MA: Hendrickson, 1989.

———. "Tradition and Citation in the Epistle of James." In *Scripture, Tradition, and Interpretation: Essays Presented to Everett F. Harrison by His Students and Colleagues in Honor of His Seventy-Fifth Birthday*, edited by W. Ward Gasque and William Sanford La Sor, 113–26. Grand Rapids: Eerdmans, 1978.

DeRoche, Michael. "Jeremiah 2:2–3 and Israel's Love for God during the Wilderness Wanderings." *CBQ* 45 (1983) 364–76.

deSilva, David A. *Honor, Patronage, Kinship and Purity: Unlocking New Testament Culture*. Downers Grove, IL: InterVarsity, 2012.

———. *The Jewish Teachers of Jesus, James, and Jude: What Earliest Christianity Learned from the Apocrypha and Pseudepigrapha*. New York: Oxford University Press, 2012.

Dibelius, Martin. *James: A Commentary on the Epistle of James*. Translated by Heinrich Greeven. Hermeneia. Philadelphia: Fortress, 1976.

Didymus the Blind. *Commentary on Zechariah*. Translated by Robert C. Hill. FC 111. Washington, DC: Catholic University of America Press, 2006.

Edgar, David. *Has God Not Chosen the Poor? The Social Setting of the Epistle of James*. JSNTSup 206. Sheffield: T&T Clark, 2001.

Edgar, David H. "The Use of the Love-Command and the Shema' in the Epistle of James." *Proceedings of the Irish Biblical Association* 23 (2000) 9–22.

Elliott, John H. "The Epistle of James in Rhetorical and Social Scientific Perspective: Holiness-Wholeness and Patterns of Replication." *BTB* 23 (1993) 71–81.

Ellis, Nicholas J. *The Hermeneutics of Divine Testing: Cosmic Trials and Biblical Interpretation in the Epistle of James and Other Jewish Literature*. WUNT 396. Tübingen: Mohr Siebeck, 2015.

Evans, Katherine G. "Friendship in the Greek Documentary Papyri and Inscriptions: A Survey." In *Greco-Roman Perspectives on Friendship*, edited by John T. Fitzgerald, 181–202. SBLRBS 34. Atlanta: Scholars Press, 1997.

Fishbane, Michael A., ed. *Haftarot: The Traditional Hebrew Text with the New JPS Translation*. JPS Bible Commentary. Philadelphia: JPS, 2002.

Foster, Robert J. *The Significance of Exemplars for the Interpretation of the Letter of James*. WUNT 376. Tübingen: Mohr Siebeck, 2014.

Francis, Fred Owens. "Form and Function of the Opening and Closing Paragraphs of James and 1 John." *ZNW* 61 (1970) 110–26.

Frick, P. "A Syntactical Note on the Dative Τῷ Κόσμῳ in James 2:5." *Filología Neotestamentaria* 17 (2004) 99–103.

Garland, David E. "Severe Trials, Good Gifts, and Pure Religion: James 1." *RevExp* 83 (1986) 383–94.

Garrett, Thomas More. "The Message to the Merchants in James 4:13–17 and Its Relevance for Today." *Journal of Theological Interpretation* 10 (2016) 299–315.

Gilbert, M. "Wisdom Literature." In *Jewish Writings of the Second Temple Period: Apocrypha, Pseudepigrapha, Qumran, Sectarian Writings, Philo, Josephus*, edited by Michael E. Stone, 283–324. CRINT. Philadelphia: Fortress, 1984.

Ginzberg, Louis. *Legends of the Jews, Volumes 1 and 2*. Edited by Henrietta Szold and Paul Radin. Philadelphia: JPS, 2003.

Gray, Patrick. "Points and Lines: Thematic Parallelism in the Letter of James and the Testament of Job." *NTS* 50 (2004) 406–24.

Guthrie, George H., and Mark E. Taylor. "The Structure of James." *CBQ* 68 (2006) 681–705.

Hartin, Patrick J. *James*. SP 14. Collegeville, MN: Liturgical Press, 2003.

———. *James and the Q Sayings of Jesus*. Sheffield: JSOT, 1991.

———. "James and the Q Sermon on the Mount/Plain." *SBLSP* 28 (1989) 440–57.

———. "The Poor in the Epistle of James and the Gospel of Thomas." *HvTSt* 53 (1997) 146–62.

———. *A Spirituality of Perfection: Faith in Action in the Letter of James*. Collegeville, MN: Liturgical Press, 1999.

———. "'Who Is Wise and Understanding among You' (Jas 3:13)? An Analysis of Wisdom, Eschatology and Apocalypticism in the Epistle of James." *HvTSt* 53 (1997) 969-99.
Hays, Richard B. *Echoes of Scripture in the Letters of Paul*. New Haven: Yale University Press, 1993.
Herman, G. "The 'Friends' of the Early Hellenistic Rulers: Servants or Officials?" *Talanta* 12 (1980) 103-49.
Hiebert, D. Edmond. *The Epistle of James: Tests of a Living Faith*. Chicago: Moody, 1979.
Hogan, Karina Martin. "Elusive Wisdom and the Other Nations in Baruch." In *The "Other" in Second Temple Judaism: Essays in Honor of John J. Collins*, edited by Daniel C. Harlow et al., 145-59. Grand Rapids: Eerdmans, 2011.
Holladay, William Lee. *The Architecture of Jeremiah 1-20*. Lewisburg, PA: Bucknell University Press, 1975.
———. *Jeremiah 1: A Commentary on the Book of the Prophet Jeremiah, Chapters 1-25*. Hermeneia. Philadelphia: Fortress, 1986.
Hubbard, David Allan. *Joel and Amos*. TOTC. Downers Grove, IL: InterVarsity, 1989.
Irwin, William H. "Fear of God, the Analogy of Friendship and Ben Sira's Theodicy." *Biblica* 76 (1995) 551-59.
Jackson-McCabe, Matt A. "Enduring Temptation: The Structure and Coherence of the Letter of James." *JSNT* 37 (2014) 161-84.
Jacobs, Irving. "Midrashic Background for James 2:21-3." *NTS* 22 (1976) 457-64.
Jobes, Karen H. "The Minor Prophets in James, 1 and 2 Peter and Jude." In *The Minor Prophets in the New Testament*, edited by Maarten J. J. Menken and Steve Moyise, 135-53. LNTS 377. New York: T&T Clark, 2009.
Johanson, Bruce C. "Definition of Pure Religion in James 1:27 Reconsidered." *ExpT* 84 (1973) 118-19.
Johnson, Luke Timothy. *Brother of Jesus, Friend of God: Studies in the Letter of James*. Grand Rapids: Eerdmans, 2004.
———. "Friendship with the World and Friendship with God: A Study of Discipleship in James." In *Brother of Jesus, Friend of God: Studies in the Letter of James*, 202-20. Grand Rapids: Eerdmans, 2004.
———. "James 3:13-4:10 and the Topos Peri Phthonou." *NovT* 25 (1983) 327-47.
———. *The Letter of James*. New Haven: Yale University Press, 2005.
———. *The Letter of James: A New Translation with Introduction and Commentary*. AB 37A. New York: Doubleday, 1995.
———. "Making Connections: The Material Expression of Friendship in the New Testament." *Interpretation* 58 (2004) 158-71.
———. "The Social World of James: Literary Analysis and Historical Reconstruction." In *Brother of Jesus, Friend of God: Studies in the Letter of James*, 101-22. Grand Rapids: Eerdmans, 2004.
———. "Taciturnity and True Religion: James 1:26-27." In *Greeks, Romans, and Christians: Essays in Honor of Abraham J. Malherbe*, edited by David L. Balch et al., 329-39. Minneapolis: Fortress, 1990.
———. "The Use of Leviticus 19 in the Letter of James." *JBL* 101 (1982) 391-401.
Kamell, Mariam. "Incarnating Jeremiah's Promised New Covenant in the 'Law' of James." *EvQ* 83 (2011) 19-28.

Kamell Kovalishyn, Mariam. "James and the Apocalyptic Wisdom." In *The Jewish Apocalyptic Tradition and the Shaping of New Testament Thought*, edited by Benjamin E. Reynolds and Loren T. Stuckenbruck, 293–306. Minneapolis: Fortress, 2017.

———. "The Prayer of Elijah in James 5: An Example of Intertextuality." *JBL* 137 (2018) 1027-45.

Karris, Robert J. "Some New Angles on James 5:13–20." *RevExp* 97 (2000) 207–19.

Kattan Gribetz, Sarit. "The Shema in the Second Temple Period: A Reconsideration." *Journal of Ancient Judaism* 6 (2015) 58–84.

Keith, Pierre. "Les destinataires de l'Épître de Jacques." *Foi et Vie* 102 (2003) 19–27.

Kloppenborg, John S. "Diaspora Discourse: The Construction of Ethos in James." *NTS* 53 (2007) 242–70.

———. "Q, Thomas, and James." In *Q, the Earliest Gospel: An Introduction to the Original Stories and Sayings of Jesus*, 98–122. Louisville: Westminster John Knox, 2008.

Kloppenborg Verbin, John S. "Patronage Avoidance in James." *HvTSt* 55 (1999) 755–94.

Konradt, Matthias. *Christliche Existenz nach dem Jakobusbrief: eine Studie zu seiner soteriologischen und ethischen Konzeption*. SUNT 22. Göttingen: Vandenhoeck & Ruprecht, 1998.

———. "The Love Command in Matthew, James and the Didache." In *Matthew, James, and Didache: Three Related Documents in Their Jewish and Christian Settings*, edited by Huub Van de Sandt and Jürgen K. Zangenberg, 271–88. Atlanta: SBL, 2008.

Konstan, David. "Friendship, Frankness and Flattery." In *Friendship, Flattery, and Frankness of Speech: Studies on Friendship in the New Testament World*, edited by John T. Fitzgerald, 7–19. Leiden: Brill, 1996.

———. *Friendship in the Classical World*. New York: Cambridge University Press, 1997.

———. "Greek Friendship." *American Journal of Philology* 117 (1996) 71–94.

———. "Patrons and Friends." *Classical Philology* 90 (1995) 328–42.

———. "Problems in the History of Christian Friendship." *Journal of Early Christian Studies* 4 (1996) 87–113.

———. "Reciprocity and Friendship." In *Reciprocity in Ancient Greece*, edited by Christopher Gill et al., 279–302. New York: Oxford University Press, 1998.

Laws, Sophie. *A Commentary on the Epistle of James*. HNTC. San Francisco: Harper & Row, 1980.

Lewis, C. S. *That Hideous Strength: A Modern Fairy-Tale for Grown-Ups*. 1945. Reprint, London: HarperCollins, 2005.

Liddell, Henry George, Robert Scott, Henry Stuart Jones, and Roderick McKenzie. *A Greek-English Lexicon*. 9th ed. Oxford: Oxford University Press, 1996.

Lied, Liv Ingeborg. *The Other Lands of Israel: Imaginations of the Land in 2 Baruch*. JSJSup 129. Leiden: Brill, 2008.

Lockett, Darian. "God and 'the World': Cosmology and Theology in the Letter of James." In *Cosmology and New Testament Theology*, edited by Jonathan T. Pennington and Sean M. McDonough, 144–56. LNTS 355. London: T&T Clark, 2008.

———. *Purity and Worldview in the Epistle of James*. LNTS 366. London: A&C Black, 2008.

———. "Strong and Weak Lines: Permeable Boundaries between Church and Culture in the Letter of James." *RevExp* 108 (2011) 391–405.

Manton, Thomas. *James*. Reprint, Crossway Classic Commentaries. Wheaton, IL: Crossway, 1995.

Marcus, Joel. "The Evil Inclination in the Epistle of James." *CBQ* 44 (1982) 606–21.

Martin, Ralph P. *James*. WBC 48. Waco, TX: Word, 1988.
Marttila, M., and M. S. Pajunen. "Wisdom, Israel and Other Nations: Perspectives from the Hebrew Bible, Deuterocanonical Literature, and the Dead Sea Scrolls." *Journal of Ancient Judaism* 4 (2013) 2–26.
Matusova, Ekaterina. *The Meaning of the Letter of Aristeas: In Light of Biblical Interpretation and Grammatical Tradition, and with Reference to Its Historical Context*. Göttingen: Vandenhoeck & Ruprecht, 2015.
Maynard-Reid, Pedrito U. *Poverty and Wealth in James*. Eugene, OR: Wipf & Stock, 2004.
Mayor, Joseph B. *The Epistle of St. James: The Greek Text with Introduction and Comments*. 2nd ed. Grand Rapids: Baker, 1978.
McCartney, Dan. *James*. BECNT. Grand Rapids: Baker Academic, 2009.
McKane, William. *A Critical and Exegetical Commentary on Jeremiah*. ICC 20. Edinburgh: T&T Clark, 1986.
McKnight, Scot. *The Letter of James*. NICNT. Grand Rapids: Eerdmans, 2011.
———. *Sermon on the Mount*. The Story of God Bible Commentary. Grand Rapids: Zondervan, 2013.
Mews, Constant J. "Cicero on Friendship." In *Friendship: A History*, edited by Barbara Caine, 65–72. 2009. Reprint, London: Routledge, 2014.
Milgrom, Jo. *The Binding of Isaac: The Akedah, a Primary Symbol in Jewish Thought and Art*. Berkeley, CA: Bibal, 1988.
Moo, Douglas J. *The Letter of James: An Introduction and Commentary*. TNTC. Grand Rapids: Eerdmans, 2009.
Motyer, J. A. *The Message of James*. BST. Leicester: Inter-Varsity, 1985.
Ng, Esther Y. L. "Father-God Language and Old Testament Allusions in James." *TynBul* 54 (2003) 41–54.
O'Donovan, Oliver. *The Desire of the Nations: Rediscovering the Roots of Political Theology*. Cambridge: Cambridge University Press, 1999.
Olyan, Saul M. *Friendship in the Hebrew Bible*. The Anchor Yale Bible Reference Library. New Haven: Yale University Press, 2017.
Painter, John, and David A. deSilva. *James and Jude*. Paideia. Grand Rapids: Baker Academic, 2012.
Perdue, Leo G. "The Social Character of Paraenesis and Paraenetic Literature." *Semeia* 50 (1990) 5–39.
———. "Paraenesis and the Epistle of James." *ZNW* 72 (1981) 241–56.
Peterson, Erik. "Der Gottesfreund: Beiträge zur Geschichte eines religiösen Terminus." *Zeitschrift für Kirchengeschichte* 42 (1923) 161–202.
Polhill, John B. "Prejudice, Partiality, and Faith: James 2." *RevExp* 83 (1986) 395–404.
Popkes, Wiard. *Der Brief des Jakobus*. Leipzig: Evangelische Verlagsanstalt, 2001.
Porter, Virgil V., Jr. "The Sermon on the Mount in the Book of James, Part 1." *BSac* 162 (2005) 344–60.
———. "The Sermon on the Mount in the Book of James, Part 2." *BSac* 162 (2005) 470–82.
Reicke, Bo. *The Epistles of James, Peter, and Jude*. AB 37. Garden City, NY: Doubleday, 1964.
Roberts, David J. III. "Definition of 'Pure Religion' in James 1:27." *ExpT* 83 (1972) 215–16.
Ropes, James Hardy. *A Critical and Exegetical Commentary on the Epistle of St. James*. ICC. New York: Charles Scribner's Sons, 1916.

Sailhamer, John. "A Wisdom Composition of the Pentateuch?" In *The Way of Wisdom: Essays in Honor of Bruce K. Waltke*, edited by J. I. Packer and Sven K. Soderlund, 15–35. Grand Rapids: Zondervan, 2000.
Sasse, H. "Κοσμέω κτλ." In *TDNT* 3:867–898. Edited by Gerhard Kittel and Gerhard Friedrich. Translated by Geoffrey William Bromiley. Grand Rapids: Eerdmans, 1985.
Scobie, Charles H. H. "Israel and the Nations: An Essay in Biblical Theology." *TynBul* 43 (1992) 283–305.
Silva, Moisés, ed. "ἀγαπάω κτλ." In *NIDNTTE* 1:102–15. Grand Rapids: Zondervan, 2014.
———. "Ἐπίσκοπος κτλ." In *NIDNTTE* 2:248–53. Grand Rapids: Zondervan, 2014.
———. "Κατασκευάζω κτλ." In *NIDNTTE* 2:642–44. Grand Rapids: Zondervan, 2014.
———. "Ψυχή κτλ." In *NIDNTTE* 4:725–34. Grand Rapids: Zondervan, 2014.
Smit, Dirk J. "Exegesis and Proclamation: 'Show No Partiality...' (James 2:1–13)." *Journal of Theology for Southern Africa* 71 (1990) 59–68.
Spicq, Ceslas. "Στηρίζω." In *Theological Lexicon of the New Testament*, translated by James D. Ernest, 3:291–95. Peabody, MA: Hendrickson, 1994.
———. "Φθόνος." In *Theological Lexicon of the New Testament*, translated by James D. Ernest, 3:200–04. Peabody, MA: Hendrickson, 1994.
Stählin, Gustav. "Φίλος, Φίλη, Φιλία." In *TDNT* 9:146–171. Edited by Gerhard Kittel and Gerhard Friedrich. Translated by Geoffrey William Bromiley. Grand Rapids: Eerdmans, 1985.
Stulac, George M. *James*. IVPNTC. Downers Grove, IL: InterVarsity, 2011.
Stulman, Louis. *Jeremiah*. AOTC. Nashville: Abingdon, 2011.
Tamez, Elsa. *The Scandalous Message of James: Faith without Works Is Dead*. 1990. Rev. ed., New York: Crossroad, 2002.
Taylor, Mark E. *A Text-Linguistic Investigation into the Discourse Structure of James*. LNTS. London: T&T Clark, 2006.
Theissen, Gerd. "Amour du prochain et égalité : Jc 2/1–13: Un moment fort de l'éthique chrétienne primitive." *ETR* 76 (2001) 325–46.
———. "Éthique et communauté dans l'Épître de Jacques: Réflexions sur son Sitz im Leben." *ETR* 77 (2002) 157–76.
Thompson, J. A. *Deuteronomy: An Introduction and Commentary*. 2nd ed. TOTC. Downers Grove, IL: IVP Academic, 2008.
Tolkien, J. R. R. *The Silmarillion*. 1977. Reprint, New York: Ballantine, 1979.
Townsend, Michael J. "James 4:1–4: A Warning against Zealotry?" *ExpT* 87 (1976) 211–13.
Trudinger, P. "The Epistle of James: Down-to-Earth and Otherworldly?" *Downside Review* 122 (2004) 61–63.
Tsuji, Manabu. *Glaube zwischen Vollkommenheit und Verweltlichung: Eine Untersuchung zur literarischen Gestalt und zur inhaltlichen Kohärenz des Jakobusbriefes*. Tübingen: Mohr Siebeck, 1997.
Varner, William. "The Main Theme and the Structure of James." *The Master's Seminary Journal* 22 (2011) 115–29.
Verboven, Koenraad. "Friendship among the Romans." In *The Oxford Handbook of Social Relations in the Roman World*, edited by Michael Peachin, 404–21. Oxford: Oxford University Press, 2011.
Verseput, Donald. "Genre and Story: The Community Setting of the Epistle of James." *CBQ* 62 (2000) 96–110.
———. "James 1:17 and the Jewish Morning Prayers." *NovT* 39 (1997) 177–91.

———. "Reworking the Puzzle of Faith and Deeds in James 2:14–26." *NTS* 43 (1997) 97–115.
Vlachos, Chris A. *James: Exegetical Guide to the Greek New Testament*. Nashville: B&H Academic, 2013.
Vyhmeister, Nancy J. "The Rich Man in James 2: Does Ancient Patronage Illumine the Text?" *Andrews University Seminary Studies* 33 (1995) 265–83.
Wachob, Wesley Hiram. *The Voice of Jesus in the Social Rhetoric of James*. SNTSMS 106. Cambridge: Cambridge University Press, 2000.
Walbank, F. W. "Monarchies and Monarchic Ideals." In *The Cambridge Ancient History. Vol. 7, pt. 1, The Hellenistic World*, edited by F. W. Walbank et al., 62–100. Rev. ed. London: Cambridge University Press, 1984.
Wall, Robert W. *Community of the Wise: The Letter of James*. New Testament in Context. Valley Forge, PA: Trinity Press International, 1997.
Ward, Roy Bowen. "Partiality in the Assembly: James 2:2–4." *HTR* 62 (1969) 87–97.
Watson, Duane Frederick. "James 2 in Light of Greco-Roman Schemes of Argumentation." *NTS* 39 (1993) 94–121.
———. "The Rhetoric of James 3:1–12 and a Classical Pattern of Argumentation." *NovT* 35 (1993) 48–64.
Weaver, Joel A. "The Heart of the Law: Love Your Neighbor (Jas 2:8–13)." *RevExp* 108 (2011) 445–51.
Westfall, Cynthia Long. "Continue to Remember the Poor: Social Justice within the Poor and Powerless Jewish Christian Communities." In *The Bible and Social Justice: Old Testament and New Testament Foundations for the Church's Urgent Call*, edited by Cynthia Long Westfall and Brian R. Dyer, 152–75. McMaster New Testament Studies. Eugene, OR: Wipf &Stock, 2015.
White, Joel. *Die Erstlingsgabe im Neuen Testament*. Tübingen: Francke, 2007.
Wick, Peter. "'You Shall Not Murder . . . You Shall Not Commit Adultery': Theological and Anthropological Radicalization in the Letter of James and in the Sermon on the Mount." In *The Decalogue in Jewish and Christian Tradition*, edited by Henning Graf Reventlow and Yair Hoffman, 88–96. LBS. New York: T&T Clark, 2011.
Wilkinson, David. *Christian Eschatology and the Physical Universe*. New York: Bloomsbury, 2010.
Williams, H. H. Drake. "Of Rags and Riches: The Benefits of Hearing Jeremiah 9:23–24 within James 1:9–11." *TynBul* 53 (2002) 273–82.
Witherington, Ben. *Jesus the Sage: The Pilgrimage of Wisdom*. Minneapolis: Fortress, 1994.
———. *Letters and Homilies for Jewish Christians: A Socio-Rhetorical Commentary on Hebrews, James and Jude*. Downers Grove, IL: IVP Academic, 2007.
Wright, Christopher J. H. *The Mission of God: Unlocking the Bible's Grand Narrative*. Downers Grove, IL: IVP Academic, 2006.

Scripture Index

OLD TESTAMENT (LXX)
Genesis

1:11	85, 93
1:26	74n21
3:17–19	86
12:3	88, 89, 91n87
15:6	8
18:7	60n75

Exodus

4:22	110n20
19:5–6	91n87
20:6	23
33:11	60

Leviticus

5:14–16	89
5:22	89
19:12–19	108n15
19:18	8
26	91n89

Numbers

11:26–29	33
15:37–41	85n65

Deuteronomy

1:13	72n15
1:15	72n15
4:6–8	72–73, 95
5:10	23
5:17–18	8n17
6:4–9	23, 85n65
7:6	110n22
7:7	73
7:9	23
9:26	110n21
10:17–18	16, 71
11:8–9	91
11:11	108n14
11:13–21	84–86, 91–94, 106–108
11:13	91
11:14	84, 85, 106n9
11:17	84, 85, 107
11:26–28	91n89
14:1	110n20
14:2	110n22
14:21	110n22
26:18–19	110n22
28–29	91n89
28:9	110n22
32:1–43	88n79
32:6	110n20
32:9	110n21

Judges

5:31	23n51

SCRIPTURE INDEX

1 Kings

17–18	82, 93
18:17–18	93n94

2 Chronicles

7:14	111n29
20:7	60

Nehemiah

1:5	23n51

Esther

1:3	49n32
1:13	49n32
2:18	49n32
3:1	49n32
6:9	49n32
13:15–16	110n21

Psalms

1:2	8n19
12:6	63n91
34:13–14	52n43
36:4	52n43
36:9	75
42:1	75
45:8	52n43
49	51
56:3	63n91
66:7	107
68:5	16
68:26	75
73	51
77:11	63n91
84:13	107
97:10	52n43
99:5	25
101:3	52n43
110:1	24–25
110:4	25n61
114:7	63n91
122:6	23n51
146:9	16

Proverbs

2:1–5	8n19
3:27–28	76–77
3:34	8, 76
6:11	75n27
8:13	52n43
10:11	75n27
13:14	75n27
14:27	75n27
17:6	27
18:4	75n27
18:21	28
27:1	76–77
27:19	45

Isaiah

5:9	8n17
12:3	75
30:19	110n22
35:7	75
40:6–7	8n17
49:10	75
56:3–8	95n100
58:11	75
62:12	110n22
66:1	25
66:18–21	95n100

Jeremiah

2:2–4:4	88–89, 108–111
2:3	87n74, 88–90, 108–111
2:5	109
2:11–13	89
2:13	75
2:14	89
2:17	89
2:18	89
2:20	110n26
2:23	89
2:27–28	89
2:31	109
2:32	109
2:34	109
3:1	110n26
3:5	109

SCRIPTURE INDEX

3:6–13	110n26
3:6	110n26
3:9	110n26
3:17	95n100
3:21	109
3:34	89
4:1–2	88, 89, 90
4:5–6:30	88n78
5:24	85n69, 106
7:1–15	111n28
7:6	111n28
9:23–24	8n17, 111
12:3	8n17, 111
12:10	110n21
14:9	111n29
17:13	75
30–31	110n26
30:8	110n26
30:20	110n26
31:4	110n26
31:9	110n20
31:20	110n20
31:21	110n26
31:31–34	90, 110

Lamentations

2:3	25

Ezekiel

23:35	35

Daniel

1:4	72n15
3:91	49n32
3:94	49n32
5:11	72n15
5:23	49n32
6:13	49n32
7:27	110n22
9:4	23n51
9:19	111n29
12:7	110n22

Hosea

3:1	35
6:3	85, 92, 106
11:1	110n20
12:1	110n22
14:10	72n15

Joel

2:22–23	85, 86n72, 92, 106
3:18	75

Amos

5:15	52n43

Micah

4:1–5	95n100

Zephaniah

2:11	95n100
3:9	95n100

Zechariah

2:6–12	110n21
8:20–22	95n100
10:1	85, 92, 93n93, 106
14:16	95n100

Malachi

1:11	95n100
3:5	35
4:5–6	93n97

APOCRYPHA

Baruch

2:15	111n29

1 Maccabees

2:18	49n32
3:38	49n32
6:10	49n32
6:14	49n32
6:28	49n32
7:6	49n32
7:8	49n32
7:15	49n32
8:20	49n34
8:31	49n34
10:16	49n34
10:19–20	49n32
10:60	49n32
10:65	49n32
11:57	49n32
12:43	49n32
13:36	49n32
15:17	49n34
15:28	49n32
15:32	49n32

2 Maccabees

1:14	49n32
1:25	110n21
6:13	63n91
7:24	49n32
8:9	49n32
10:13	49n32
10:38	63n91
14:11	49n32
14:15	110n21
15:24	110n22

Ben Sirach

1:10	23n51
5:5–17	47
6:5	47
6:7	47
6:8–12	47
6:8–10	45
6:14–16	47
6:14	45
6:17	46
10:25	72n15
13:21–23	21n42
17:17–18	110n21
21:13	75n27
21:15	72n15
22:23	45
27:16	45
36:14	84n61
37:5–6	45
38:34	84n61

Tobit

13:12	23n51
14:7	23n51

Wisdom of Solomon

3:5	63n91
7:27	60, 61n83
9:2	84n61
13:5	84n61
14:11	84n61
16:2	63, 63n91
16:11	63n91

OLD TESTAMENT PSEUDEPIGRAPHA

2 Baruch

29:1	85n70

1 Enoch

10:19	86n73
71:15	31n86

3 Enoch

44:10	110n20

4 Ezra

6:58	110n20
7:43	31n86
7:50	31n86
8:1	31n86

Jubilees

2:20	110n20
17:16	66
19:9	60n76
19:29	110n20
30:21	60n78

Liber antiquitatum biblicarum

18:5	66n99
18:6	110n20
32:2–4	66n99
32:16	110n20

Letter of Aristeas

190	63n92
210	63n92
281	63n92

3 Maccabees

2:6	110n22
5:11	84n61
6:3	110n21

4 Maccabees

14:20	66n99

Psalms of Solomon

6:6	23n51
14:1	23n51
14:5	110n21

Testament of the Twelve Patriarchs

Testament of Benjamin 5:1	79n39
Testament of Simeon 3:3	38n117

Testament of Abraham

1:6	60n76
2:3	60n76
4:7	60n76
8:2	60n76
8:4	60n76
9:7	60n76
15:12	60n76
15:13	60n76
15:14	60n76
16:5	60n76
16:9	60n76
20:14	60n76

Testament of Job

1:1	81n49
4:3–5:1	81n50
11	77–79
11:3	78
27:4	81n49

NEW TESTAMENT

Matt

5:12	81n48
5:14–16	72
5:21–22	38n115
5:34–35	25n61
6:24	35n102, 36n107
8:21–22	66n101
10:34–38	66n101
12:46–50	66n101
19:29	66n101
22:44	25n61
23:8–10	66n101
23:29–39	81n48
26:64	25n61

Mark

12:36	25n61

Luke

6:22–26	81n48
11:5–8	45
11:46–52	81n48
13:33–35	81n48
16:14	34n100
20:42	25n61

SCRIPTURE INDEX

John

12:6	34n100
13:35	72n13
15:13	45n12
17:23	72n13

Acts

2:34	25n61
2:44–45	44n10
4:32–37	44n10, 72n13
5:12–13	72n13
7:51–53	81n48
8:20	34n100

Romans

8:18	31n86
8:23	83n57
8:34	25n61
11:3–4	81n48
11:16	83n57, 87n74
12:2	31n86
12:9	52n43
16:5	83n57

1 Corinthians

1:26	31n86
2:6–7	31n86
2:15	31n84
10:1–6	92n90
15:20	83n57
15:23	83n57
15:25	25n61
15:44	31n84
15:46	31n84
16:15	83n57

2 Corinthians

4:18	31n86

Galatians

1.4	31n86
6:9	77n

Ephesians

1:20	25n61

Colossians

3:5	36n107

1 Thessalonians

2:14–16	81n48
3:13	80n44
5:21–22	52n43

2 Thessalonians

2:3	83n57
2:13	87n74
3:3	80n44

1 Timothy

4:4	84n61
6:5–10	34n100

Titus

1:11	34n100

Hebrews

1:3	25n61
1:13	25n61
4:1–3	92n90
5:6	25n61
6:20	25n61
7:17	25n61
7:21	25n61
8:1	25n61
10:12–13	25n61

James

1:1	82, 86n73, 90, 109
1:2–4	65–66, 82
1:5	30, 34, 41, 65
1:6–8	32
1:6	40n123
1:8	32, 71

SCRIPTURE INDEX

Reference	Pages
1:9–11	8n17, 17, 22, 73, 79n40, 111
1:9	8n17
1:10	40n123
1:11	17n24
1:12	17, 23, 52, 65–66, 87, 96, 106
1:13–27	14n14
1:16	14n14
1:17	40n123, 51, 65, 84, 109
1:18	15, 30, 41, 52n41, 83–84, 90, 96, 108–11
1:19	14
1:20	14–15
1:21–25	77, 89, 96
1:21	14–15, 29n76, 30, 53, 65, 90
1:22	14–15
1:24–25	109
1:25	17, 70
1:26–27	11–18, 35, 55
1:26	11–15, 51
1:27	16–18, 36, 52, 55, 57, 62, 71, 109
2:1–13	16, 19–20, 38, 62, 64n93
2:1	19
2:2–4	57
2:3	24–25
2:4	21
2:5	19–26, 36, 52, 71, 73, 79n40, 106
2:6–7	26
2:8	8, 23, 52, 57, 67, 71, 77
2:11	8n17
2:12–13	87
2:12	23, 70
2:13	57, 94n98
2:14–26	77
2:14–16	71, 75
2:14	13n13
2:15	57
2:17	13n13
2:19	67, 77, 106
2:20	13n13
2:21	66, 74
2:22	65
2:23	8, 65
2:25	74
2:26	13n
3:1–12	28
3:1	34, 87, 95
3:2	13, 28
3:3–4	15, 28
3:4	52n41
3:5	28
3:6–8	28
3:6	26–30, 37, 51
3:8	13, 28
3:9	40, 57, 62, 74, 76
3:10–12	40n123, 57, 75–76
3:10	74n21
3:11	30n81, 75
3:13–4:10	33, 62
3:13–18	14, 29, 33, 57, 72
3:13	34
3:14	30n81, 31, 75
3:15	30–32, 37, 39, 50n36
3:16	31
3:17	13, 29, 41, 53, 70–71, 96
4:1–10	30, 32–34
4:1–4	51, 63
4:1–3	37
4:1–2	14, 33, 37, 65
4:1	37, 51
4:2	37
4:3	33, 37
4:4	31, 32–38, 50–52, 58, 81
4:5	33, 65, 96
4:6–5:6	32, 37, 76
4:6	8, 32, 41, 51, 62, 76
4:7	36
4:8	32, 37, 52
4:11–12	14, 25, 57, 67, 87, 96, 106
4:13–17	57, 76–79, 94
4:13	77–78
4:14	22, 40n123, 79n40
4:17	71, 76–77
5:1–6	79, 94
5:4	8n17
5:5	111
5:6	32, 37n, 58, 76n31, 82
5:7–18	84–86, 91–94, 96, 106–108

SCRIPTURE INDEX

James (continued)

5:7–11	78n, 80–82, 92
5:7–8	66, 87, 96
5:7	40, 80, 86n72, 92
5:8	80, 92
5:9	86, 87, 92n91, 94n98
5:10	80, 81
5:11	66, 80, 82, 92n92, 96
5:12	15, 87, 94n98
5:13	57
5:14–15	93
5:15	65, 66, 80n43
5:16	82
5:17	74
5:18	40
5:19–20	96
5:19	57

1 Peter

3:3	10n2, 27n68
3:10–11	52n43
5:10	80n44

2 Peter

2:3	34n100

1 John

2:17	31n86

Jude

11	34n100
19	31n84

Revelations

2:2	52n43
3:2	80n44
5:13	84n61
8:9	84n61
11:17–18	81n48
14:4	83n57, 87n74
16:5–6	81n48
18:21–19:2	81n48

21:16	85n70

JEWISH TEXTS

Philo

Abr. (*On the Life of Abraham*)

87	60n76
167	66
170	66n99
198	66n99
235	60n76
273	60n76

Conf. (*On the Confusion of Tongues*)

98	25n58

Congr. (*On the Preliminary Studies*)

38	63n89
97	63n89
171	63n89

Decal. (*On the Decalogue*)

41	63n89

Det. (*That the Worse Attacks the Better*)

33	46

Deus (*That God Is Unchangeable*)

4	66n99
110	63n89

Ebr. (*On Drunkenness*)

94	60n77

Her. (Who Is the Heir?)

19–21	61
21	48n30, 60n78
83	46

Hypot. (Hypothetica)

11.4	45
11.10–13	45

Leg. (Allegorical Interpretation)

1:96	63n89
2:56	63n89
3:1	60n78
3:71	60
3:74	60n78
3:137	63n89
3:204	60, 60n78

Migr. (On the Migration of Abraham)

45	60n77
116	48n30

Moses (On the Life of Moses)

1:155–157	61
1:156	60n77
2:256	63n89

Mut. (On the Change of Names)

28	63n89

Opif. (On the Creation of the World)

169	63n89

Plant. (On Planting)

87	63n89
90	63n89
106	45

Post. (On the Posterity of Cain)

154	63n89

Prob. (That Every Good Person Is Free)

42	60n78, 61
44	60n78
45	61, 65
85–88	45

Sacr. (On the Sacrifices of Cain and Abel)

127	63n89
130	60n77

Sobr. (On Sobriety)

50	63n89
55–56	61
56	60n76
57	61, 65
58	63n89

Somn. (On Dreams)

1:163	63n89
2:219	60n78
2:296	60
2:297	60n78

Spec. (On the Special Laws)

1:152	63n89
1:209	63n89
1:221	63n89
1:272	63n89
1:300	63n89
2:219	63n89
4:180	83n57

Virt. (On the Virtues)

103	46
218	60n76, 66n99

Josephus

Antiquities

1.13.1	66n99

War

1.21.2	84n61
1.21.7	84n61
2.6.1	84n61

Mishnah

Bikkurim

3	83n56

Babylonian Talmud

Sanhedrin

113a	93n93

Jerusalem Talmud

Sanhedrin

10:28b	93n93

Targum Onqelos

Genesis 49:12	86n73

Targum Neofiti

Genesis 18:7	60n75

Genesis Rabbah

55:7	66n99
56:4	66n99
56:8	66n99
56:10	66n99

GRECO-ROMAN WRITINGS

Aristotle

Eth. Eud. (Eudemian Ethics)

7.2.15–17	46
7.2.46	47
7:4	48
7.6.10	45n14
7:8	48
7:10	48

Eth. Nic. (Nichomachean Ethics)

8.1	45
8.2	44, 46
8.3	46
8.4	46
8:5	48
8:8	48
8.14.3	21n42
9.4	45n14
9.8.2	44, 45
9.9.7	46

Rhet. (Rhetoric)

2.5.7	21n42

Cicero

Amic. (On Friendship)

4.14	45n15
5.18	46
7.24	45, 45n12
17.62	47
17.63	47
27.100	46
27.105	43

Epictetus

Diatr. (Diatribes)

2.17.27	59n73
4.3.9	59n73

Plutarch

Adul. amic. (*How to Tell a Flatterer from a Friend*)

6	45n15

Amic. mult. (*On Having Many Friends*)

3–5	46n21
3	45, 46n19
8	45n14, 45n15

EARLY CHRISTIAN WRITINGS

1 Clement

10:1	60n76
17:2	60n76
29:2	110n21
29:3	83n57
36:5	25n58
59:3	63n90

Acts of John

108:1	63n90

Acts of Philip

35:2	63n90

Acts of Pilate

9:2	63n90

Didache

11:3–12	34n100

Epistle of Barnabas

12:10	25n58
14:4	110n21
16:2	25n58

Hermas

17:2	84n61
38:1	84n61
47:3	84n61

Irenaeus

Haer. (*Against Heresies*)

4.14.4	60n76
4.16.2	60n76
5.33.3	85n70, 86n73

Origen

Homilies on Genesis

8.2	66n99

Tertullian

Adv. Jud. (*Against the Jews*)

2:7	60n76

www.ingramcontent.com/pod-product-compliance
Lightning Source LLC
Chambersburg PA
CBHW071439160426
43195CB00013B/1970